D1432959

Practical
Leatherwork

Cutting, Sewing,
Finishing, and Repair

CARSTEN BOTHE

4880 Lower Valley Road • Atglen, PA 19310

Original edition edited by Helge Wittkopp & Ulrike Reihn-Hamburger
Original edition composition and design by gbs-Mediendesign, Königswinter

English edition cover design by Justin Watkinson
Photographs: Archives of the author
With the exception of:
© Kais Bodensieck, www.fotodesign-xtrascharf.de: pp. 17, 19, 53–55, 58, 66, 77, 81–83, 85
© Fotolia.com: haveseen (book cover 1, bottom), Eky Chan (book cover 1, center), WoGi (book cover 1, top), 123creativecom (book jacket 4, background), emevil (pp. 4, 5), leungchopan (p. 6), Teodora_D (p. 8), Maurizio Targhetta (p. 11), The Tannery in Fez, Morocco (p. 12), leungchopan (p. 31), Teodora_D (pp. 36, 38, 39), hanki-mage9 (p. 42), zonch (p. 46), Africa Studio (pp. 62, 86), javier brosch (p. 80, top), ulkan (p. 92), Scott Sanders (p. 102)

Type set in Helvetica Neue

ISBN: 978-0-7643-5744-2
Printed in China

Published by Schiffer Publishing, Ltd.
4880 Lower Valley Road
Atglen, PA 19310
Phone: (610) 593-1777; Fax: (610) 593-2002
E-mail: Info@schifferbooks.com
Web: www.schifferbooks.com

For our complete selection of fine books on this and related subjects, please visit our website at www.schifferbooks.com. You may also write for a free catalog.

Schiffer Publishing's titles are available at special discounts for bulk purchases for sales promotions or premiums. Special editions, including personalized covers, corporate imprints, and excerpts, can be created in large quantities for special needs. For more information, contact the publisher.

We are always looking for people to write books on new and related subjects. If you have an idea for a book, please contact us at proposals@schifferbooks.com.

Foreword

Dear reader,

Everyone uses products made of leather, regardless of whether you are a hunter, horseback rider, dog handler, bushcraft fan, or Boy or Girl Scout. Often, however, they get worn out and must be repaired or even manufactured anew. Leather is a natural material, and it is a real pleasure to work with. Unfortunately, there is barely any suitable literature in the German-speaking world that I could read to learn about how to work with leather. I had to teach myself—at that time still as a student—the basic things on my own. Now I am very happy to be able to pass this knowledge and these skills on to you. Sewing leather is very easy, and you can quickly achieve presentable results. A beginner should at least be able to finish a good belt within an hour.

In this little book, you will learn what a seam is all about, and could start on simple projects right away. This should lay the foundation for you to be able to also acquire the theoretical knowledge as well as the handicraft skills over time. Perhaps you will then add on carving or painting leather, so that the finished workpiece also emerges as a work of art.

If you have been able to master this little book well or if you still have unanswered questions, I would be glad to get your feedback, because then this passage can be changed in the next edition.

With warm regards,

Yours, Carsten Bothe

Contents

Fundamentals 37

Marking and Cutting Out Leather 43

A Simple Seam 47

Projects 63

Leather-Crafting Materials

Workplace and Materials

THE WORKPLACE

Most hobby leather crafters start out as knife makers and then try to make the leather sheath in their knife workshop. Unfortunately, the dust caused by the grinding work flies through the air everywhere and then accumulates on the leather. The metal filing or grinding dust then combines with hand sweat and tannin to make an insoluble black iron gall ink and leaves permanent black spots on the leather. For this reason you should outsource your leather workshop at the earliest possible stage of your hobby. This will prevent poor-quality results and disappointments caused by poor-quality surroundings. Sewing leather is a very clean activity, so much so that it can be done "at the kitchen table." At least, this is better than having to completely vacuum the entire workshop before doing the actual work.

As a support you need a stable table with a clean surface, so that you do not soil the leather. If you want to work on entire hides, you should use a table with a front at least 8 feet (2.5 m) long that is at least 3.3 feet (1 m) wide. For cutting, you need a pad that is available in craft shops. This is a green plastic mat that does not dull your knife and has a surface that closes up again after you make a cut. As a result, you always have a smooth surface available and can cut through the leather cleanly down to the last fiber.

Sewing leather is a very clean activity.

As a support for cutting, you will need a green plastic "craft mat" and a piece of waste wood.

However, you cannot under any circumstances use these mats for punching holes with a drive punch, since they can then be perforated very quickly. Using thick pieces of waste wood works well for this work; you can dispose of them as soon as the wood surface becomes too worn out. On the other hand, a heavy and smooth stone slab is ideal for punching; for example, a marble or granite window sill works well for this.

If you set up a fixed leather workplace, then the available light is an important factor. If you rely exclusively on daylight, then part of your workpiece on the lacing-stitching pony will always be in the dark, due to its design. A proper neon or LED tube with sufficient lighting helps you see clearly, which is extremely helpful when threading the needles. Bright walls reflect the light and thus make your work enjoyable. For hobby leather crafters especially, who pursue their passion mainly in the evening after work—as well as in winter, and thus mostly after sunset—artificial lighting is indispensable.

Different types of processing or tanning are used for leather.

THE LEATHER
Tanning and Types of Leather

There are different types of processing or tanning used on leather: leather with hair is referred to as a hide or a pelt (pelt tanning or pelt preparation). These types are rarely used in leather sewing, because this comes under the scope of furrier's work. It is necessary to use a special furrier's sewing machine to work on this soft leather, and in addition it must be glued to a backing material, since otherwise the thin leather and the fragile seams would tear open during wear.

A hide that neither has any hair nor is tanned is called rawhide or parchment. It is extremely difficult and rather unusual to work with this material. Rawhide is occasionally used only as a material for making braided belts.

A hide without hair and a grain side that has been tanned with oil or fish oil and has been buffed until it is soft is called chamois leather. It is mainly used for traditional clothing. You can work with it like fabric, using good industrial sewing machines. For long seams, a band of fabric is glued on to prevent the leather from being torn and pushed out of shape by the sewing machine. Small pieces that you use to make a bag or moccasins can also be sewn by hand, using a round awl.

The material that I deal with primarily in this book is saddle leather, also called sleeked or harness leather. It has a grain or skin side; only the hair has already been removed. Depending on how it is tanned, the leather is more or less stiff. As the experts say, "it has stance" if it is not so easy to

bend. The surface is smoothed and greased to a varying extent or coated with wax.

Thin, soft hides with a grain side (with the hair side outward) are called nappa leather, with a napped grain side to make suede. You can use an industrial sewing machine to work with it, and it is usually chrome tanned. However, this tanning process can cause the leather to become uncomfortable to wear if it comes into contact with moisture such as sweat. In addition, the leather also dyes readily.

HOW DO YOU FIND GOOD LEATHER?

In the last twenty years, leather crafters—like many craftsmen—have become fewer and fewer in number, and along with this, the requirement for good saddle leather has become less and less. Fortunately, the growing popularity of knife making, the live-action role-playing (LARP) scene, and the bushcraft movement has compensated for this situation in recent years. If it was twenty years ago, you would still be in this predicament of only being able to buy exclusively in large quantities to equip your leather workshop; today the internet is full of mail order companies that supply leather in quantities for normal household use. As soon as you touch the leather, you will notice immediately whether it is the right leather: it must be slightly greasy due to the presence of the right kinds of oils, and in any case it must be vegetable tanned. Chrome tanning is not suitable for our purposes. The leather pieces should be between 0.12 and 0.24 inches (3–6 mm) thick and not have too much "stance," meaning it should not

Depending on how it is tanned, the leather is more or less stiff.

be too hard. In most cases, the product description will already state what the leather in question is suitable for. It is even better if you describe to the seller—if you are able select suitable pieces on the spot—what you are planning to do and what you expect from the leather. Do not be shy about complaining about or returning the leather if it does not meet your requirements. Otherwise you will remain annoyed for years, while the leather lies on your shelf at home and you always have to reach around it. The work is worth doing only with perfect leather.

The work is worth doing only with perfect leather.

Leather is of interest only in natural colors—meaning only white—or lightly dyed to a light brown. Already dyed pieces in the most beautiful neon or parrot colors are usually treated with a lot of chemicals, which is unnecessary. You should dye the pieces yourself and then treat them with leather care products, so you can control the coloring and you can also make workpieces in several colors from a piece of light-colored leather. Otherwise you would have to spend a lot of money to buy half a hide each time, just to make a belt or a knife sheath.

You can buy belt blanks already cut out in different widths, lengths, and thicknesses.

You can buy belt blanks already cut out in various widths, lengths, and thicknesses. This way, you can gain your first experience in leather craft while investing just a little money (see page 64).

A leather that works especially well for making Nordic- or Scandinavian-style leather sheaths is a relatively thin leather, not more than 0.12 inches (3 mm) thick, which has a "spit"—an untanned layer in the middle. This leather is soaked in water before it is processed and draws together somewhat as it dries. To make the sheath fit exactly later on, either sew around a wooden last—measured to the sheath—or use the knife wrapped in plastic wrap. Sewing this leather is rather comparable to using chamois-tanned leather; you likewise use a curved awl and needles, because the two leather edges are sewn edge to edge or where it is bent. But this is something for professionals and beyond the scope of this book.

THE THREAD
Natural and Man-Made Materials

When dealing with the subject of "sewing leather," the thread used is often woefully neglected. Yet, it is just as important as the leather itself because a good seam holds just as long as the leather does. There are many man-made and natural materials used for stitching. Man-made materials include florist's wire or brass wire for serious or emergency repairs, as well as artificial sinews, nylon thread, and others. Natural stitching materials are made from genuine animal sinews, rawhide, strips of leather, and thread made from plant materials.

Threads made of synthetic fibers are the best choice for making a craftsmanlike, clean artisan seam. Unfortunately, nowadays it is getting ever harder to get the right kind, and, above all, material that is thick enough. Even though many kinds of thread made of natural materials are available, these are rarely twisted in the traditional way but, rather, are braided on modern machines. This has the disadvantage that you cannot trim this thread to a point at the end and skillfully thread it through a needle. This kind of thread is also usually made of cotton, which does not wear as well as hemp or linen.

TWISTED AND BRAIDED THREAD

Braided thread—also known as *Forellenfäden* (trout line) in German—is smoother and more uniform than twisted thread on the surface, so it is better to work with when using a sewing machine. If you use a strong magnifying glass, you can immediately recognize the braid pattern. If you take a centimeter or so of the braided thread between your thumb and forefinger and rotate it counterclockwise, it still holds together. The twisted thread, on the other hand, splits apart into its various strands when it is rotated.

The drawback of all braided thread— whether man-made or natural—is that it cannot be trimmed to a point properly. As a result, the thread goes through the needle eye in a double thickness, so that the hole in the leather has to be pierced unnecessarily large. Especially when you sew two stitches back to finish the seam, such a thing is very annoying. However, a cleanly pointed thread is not much thicker in the eye than the rest of the thread. Apart from this, leather—especially in the vegetable-tanned form—is a natural material with which it is best to use a plant fiber, with tree resin and beeswax rubbed in. Crafting high-quality leather while making a craftsmanlike seam succeeds only if you use the appropriate stitching material.

Knife owners often try to use wire to mend a seam that is cut through at the tip of the sheath, in the hope that the knife won't stick through it any more. The reason for the damage, however, is not poor stitching material, but rather the incorrect design of the sheath. Metal should never be used as a stitching material on leather, so any discussion of this material is already closed.

An artificial sinew is a kind of thread made of a flat, waxed plastic strip that can be split into many

When dealing with the subject of "sewing leather," the thread used is often woefully neglected. Yet, it is just as important as the leather itself because a good seam holds just as long as the leather does.

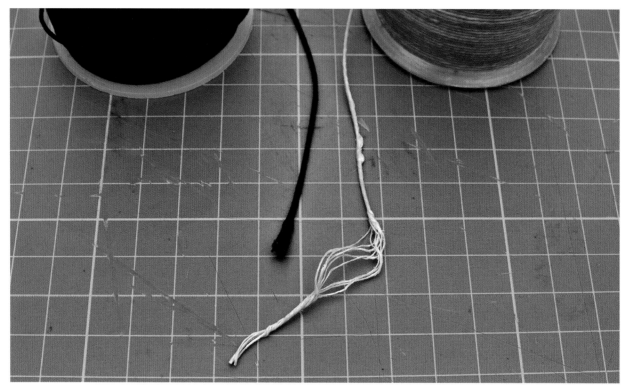

The left thread consists of braided single threads; the right thread is twisted and can be easily untwisted into single threads and can also be trimmed to a point.

thin, parallel fibers. This way you are able to draw off the thickness you need each time. Artificial sinew is used, for example, in Indian pearl embroidery, since it is very durable and tear resistant. Artificial sinew is used less frequently to sew smooth leather than it is to sew chamois leather for clothing.

Rawhide is intended for sewing saddle trees or heavily stressed parts of saddles. However, it can also be used for knife sheaths or holsters. The material is very stiff and rigid. Karl May wrote that

> **TIP**
> You can fuse raw threads with a lot of protruding fibers with a lighter.

the Indians would wet it to tie up their prisoners; as it dried, the leather then contracts. However, we cannot make use of this effect when sewing because it would make the leather spotty. To process rawhide, it is stretched over a sharp edge, and this makes it supple. At the same time it becomes whitish and is no longer so translucent. If you use enough leather grease, sewing becomes relatively easy. The stitches must be set closer together on the curves, so that the overlaps continue to appear consistent. The work is worth it, however, because rawhide that has been sewn to overlap will almost never fray. Rawhide is not used for normal seams, but only for sewing around edges. Since it is very hard to come by strips that will match, this material is not widely available in

Easy to see on a flea market find: "Repair" using wire.

It not only is difficult to obtain rawhide for sewing, but besides this, it is a material for specialists.

When sewing rawhide strips, the stitches must be set parallel to the leather edge.

Germany. Rawhide is the material traditionally used for making hand-braided cowboy lassos, which are called lariats.

Polyester thread is braided into a round shape and is very tear resistant, and you can get it in the most-beautiful colors. It is particularly popular among beginners, even if it is hard to trim to a point and to thread into the needle. After it is knotted, the ends are melted together using a lighter, so that the knot cannot come untied again. Polyester thread absorbs wax and pine pitch very poorly.

Strips of leather are often used as a stitching material to make carved leather western holsters and saddles, on which the edges are not only stitched up but are decorated at the same time by the visual effect of the braiding. It is not easy to sew with strips of leather, but it's an art in itself. Any uneven spacing between the holes and untidy work is immediately noticeable. In addition, a leather strip wears through quickly, and therefore the seam does not last as long as a seam sewn with thread.

Waxed dental floss is frequently touted as a suitable stitching material for leather, but it definitively is nothing of the kind, because it is much too thin. It is certainly possible to make emergency repairs using it, but for making new leather goods you should rely on a sensible stitching material. Meanwhile, there are a lot of good materials available on the internet.

PREPARING THE THREAD

Preparing a natural thread for sewing is actually quite simple, but this skill is little known. On the basis of the saying "long thread—lazy girl," cut off an arm-span length plus about a hand width of thread. Later, you will thread needles onto both ends of the thread. First of all, if you have a particularly raw piece of thread, you can singe off the excess fibers by using a lighter, then trim the two ends of the thread to a point. To do this, pull one end under the blade of the leather knife, separating it into fibers and thinning it out. Split about three finger widths into fibers, so it then looks like a fan. Use the same process on the other end of the thread. Now rub plenty of pine pitch into the entire thread. To do this, hang it on a nail on the wall or from a hook at the work table and quickly rub a lump of pitch along the thread, so that the friction heat makes the pitch soft. It impregnates the thread and makes the seam adhere to the leather. Change the contact point on the nail so that you can also rub the middle part of the thread. Finally, pull the two ends through the pitch and at the same time

To process rawhide, it is stretched over a sharp edge, and this makes it supple.

Preparing a natural thread for sewing is actually quite simple, but this skill is little known.

Cut off a sufficient length of thread. Then press the cobbler's knife blade on the last hand width of thread and pull it through under the blade. At the same time, only some of the material should be scraped off the fibers.

The scraped-off fibers remain hanging on the blade. This gives the thread a point.

Do the same on the other end as well.

Draw the ends through a lump of wax several times.

trim the ends to a point. Now the thread is very sticky, so that it is difficult to pull it through the leather. To make it smoother again, repeat the whole process with a lump of beeswax. You can also use special saddle wax, which already contains a mixture of pine pitch and beeswax; if you do so, you need to treat the thread only a single time. When finished, you should have a perfectly impregnated and ready-made thread in front of you.

Now all that you need are the needles: In the past they would insert a hog's bristle; today we use either steel bristles (thin steel wire folded and soldered together along four-fifths of its length) or saddle needles with a blunt tip. At a hand's width away from the pointed end, twirl the thread so that it comes apart in the middle, so you can stick the tip of the needle through it. Then twist the thread again and open out the thread another time, about one finger width away from the first spot, so that you can stick the needle through here as well. Thread the pointed end of the thread into the eye of the needle and pull it out again. Now the thread is through the

eye, and the needle has pierced it twice. Hold the needle firmly by the shaft and pull the long end of the thread upward through the eye and away, so that the pointed end is caught by the loops—which are produced by piercing the thread. This all sounds more complicated than it is. Just get your bearings from the pictures. This method fastens the thread firmly to the needle, and it can no longer slide out. Furthermore, due to the thinning, there are no thick junctions, but it can easily slip through the hole in the leather. A thick layer of beeswax helps in the sewing later on. Using pine pitch is unnecessary because the first bit of thread on the needle is not used for the seam but serves as a grip to pull the thread tight. Finally, cut off the ends and discard them.

The needles serve to thread only the thin end of the thread through the holes in the leather; you pull just on the thread itself, which is the reason that it must be long enough. Calculate it at eight times the length of the seam plus the added amount for the ends, which you need to pull the thread tight.

TIP

Have enough needles ready, because often you need to stitch only a short seam of eight to ten stitches, and can avoid having to use another new thread.

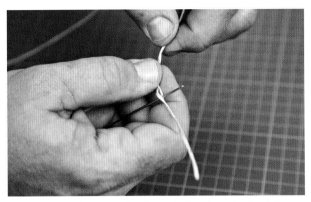

Stick the tip of the needle through the thread, about three or four finger widths away from the end.

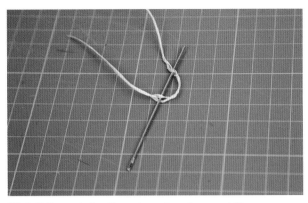

Stick it through the thread, again a finger width away.

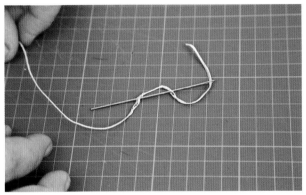

Thread the pointed end of the thread through the eye of the needle.

Pull the long end of the thread upward and draw the pointed end as far through the eye as it will go.

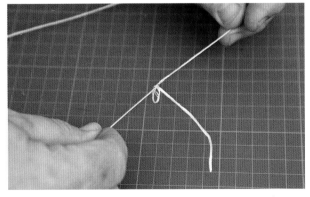

Pull the long thread completely through the eye, so that the two ends make a loop.

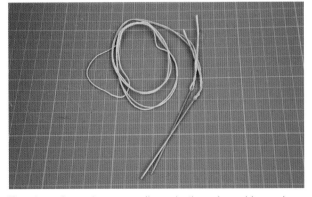

The thread now has a needle on both ends and is ready for sewing.

The Tools

The cobbler's knife is the most important cutting tool.

Round knives work very well for making long, straight cuts.

COBBLER'S KNIFE

The so-called cobbler's knife is likely the most important cutting tool; it consists of a thin sheet-metal blade with a diagonally shaped cutting edge that is sharpened on one side. For me, these thin and quite flexible blades were always too "wobbly," and they are also difficult to guide, so that for several decades already I have been making my own model from a through-hardened machine metal saw blade. To do this, use an angle grinder to cut the saw blade at an angle, clamp it in a vice so that the jaws hold a good part of it, and strike the part standing up with a hammer. Cutting through the entire blade with a grinder would generate too much heat. Then grind the cutting edge into shape and whip-stitch around the shaft with some leather. The blade should be sharpened from the right side for anyone who is right-handed, and from the left side for anyone who is left-handed. Using this tool, you can cut along a line drawn on the material without the cut running untrue.

ROUND KNIFE

A round knife works well for making long and straight cuts. You can use it either to cut off short pieces, as when using a chopper with a curved blade, or to run the entire knife along a ruler and thus execute long and straight cuts. First insert the tip of the blade and push it slightly forward. When the blade then slides into the leather, tilt the knife so that you are cutting with the rounded edge and no longer with the tip. This way, a lot of the cutting edge is applied to the leather at an extremely flat angle, which is the reason for the excellent cutting performance.

COBBLER'S HAMMER

A cobbler's hammer works well to hammer seams flat and to bind pieces of leather together. It is particularly important is make sure that the face of the hammer, which should be slightly curved outward, is absolutely clean and polished. Nicks and spots of rusts would leave stains on the leather or damage it and should therefore be prevented at all costs.

WING DIVIDER

For marking wide hole intervals on leather, such as for making a belt, a wing divider works well. You can also do this using a normal school compass, but not as well, since the tip is too thin and therefore hard to see. To be able to work comfortably and accurately, using the professional tool is recommended in any case.

EDGE BEVELER

You can also bevel the edges with a knife, but the work can be done better and more evenly using an edge beveler. This is pushed along the edge and cuts off a long and uniform leather thread. In order to obtain a neat result when making belts, you should fasten a board to the table with a screw clamp, on which you can lay the cut piece of leather. To resharpen an edge beveler, simply hold the side that faces the leather up to a running buffing wheel, applying polishing wax, and the blade is sharp again right away.

STITCHING GROOVER

To prevent the seam from fraying because it lies on top of the leather, it should be recessed. To do this, you have to cut a groove out of the leather by using a stitching groover.

The stitching groover is adjustable and uses the leather edge as a guide. You can also work freehand with it, but only if the line has been neatly marked beforehand, because if you make a wrong cut, it is not easy to correct it again. This work can also be done without a stitching groover. To do this, use a cobbler's knife to cut a narrow V-shaped groove out of the leather. But the work goes better and faster when you use the right tool.

The thinner the leather, the thinner and closer to the edge the groove should be.

Use a stitching groover to chamfer a groove for recessing the seam parallel to the edge of the leather.

GROOVING TOOL

An edge on leather looks professional only when you press a groove into the leather, parallel to the edge. You can buy a grooving tool for this purpose or make one of bone or hardwood yourself. What is important is that you have different intervals and groove widths available. The thinner the leather, the closer to the edge and the narrower the groove should be. Rub along the marked groove with little pressure and then go over this line several times, while increasing the speed and pressure steadily. In this way you avoid slipping out of it, and the groove becomes deeper and darker until it pleases you.

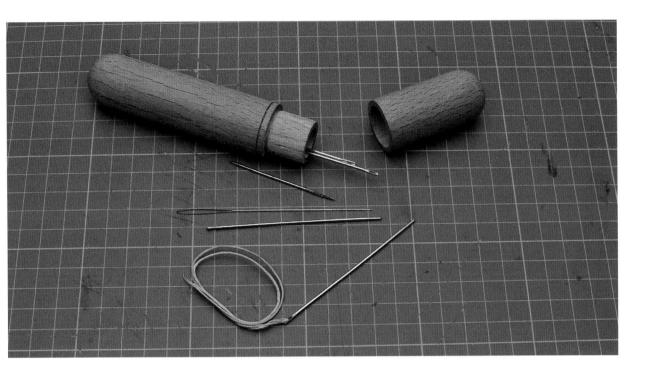

NEEDLES

Needles are used when sewing leather only to draw the thread through the already prepierced hole. Therefore, typical leather needles are blunt. This has the additional advantage that the thread will not be damaged when you sew back over two stitches at the end of the seam.

The needles with a triangular, pointed tip are designed for very thin, soft clothing leather or for furriers. They are also suitable for mending cracks in clothing leather. To stick such needles through the leather, you need at least a thimble or, even better, a saddlery glove, since otherwise you can stab the dull end of the needle into your finger.

In the past, people used hog's bristles instead of needles; these were attached to the end of the pointed threads with pine pitch. This is rarely done today. As an alternative, there are steel bristles that are each made of a double-laid steel wire that is soldered to the shaft. These bristles are attached to the thread like needles.

Needles are inexpensive, so you should always have a small supply ready, because if one gets lost you usually don't have a replacement at home and your work is held up. It also makes sense to have several threads already prepared, so that when you are sewing longer seams you don't have to interrupt the work flow to "reload" the needles.

Typical leather needles are blunt because the holes are prepierced using an awl.

LACING-STITCHING PONY

To make a neat seam, the workpiece must be firmly clamped. For this purpose, a lacing-stitching pony, also called a *Krokodilmaul* (crocodile's jaws) in German, is ideal. This can be screwed to a table, clamped in a vice, or held tight with your thighs on a "cobbler's bench." Using two simple boards, to which two slats have been screwed on the inside, and a leather strap as a hinge, you can improvise a simple lacing-stitching pony. Clamp it into a vice and it is all you need for small pieces. Do not clamp it too tightly, however, so that you avoid leaving imprints on the leather.

BONE FOLDER

A bone folder is a genuinely universal tool for the leather crafter. Using the tip, you can press patterns or decorations into the hair side of the leather or easily "mark out" a cut. If you have made a mistake when doing this, simply remove the line with the blunt end of the bone folder. With the smooth shaft you can polish the edges of the leather. On wet-formed leather, use the blunt end to press on the leather in the corners and indentations. When buying a bone folder, you should pay attention that in any case you buy one made of bone, because the ones made of plastic do not work that well.

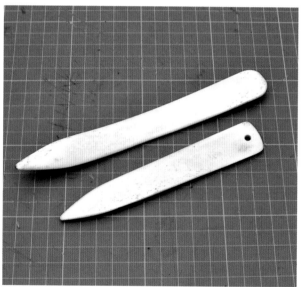

Bone folders of bone work better than plastic ones.

SPOKESHAVE FOR LEATHER

A leather spokeshave with replaceable razor blades is a practical tool if you have to thin out larger pieces of leather. However, since this is only rarely to be found, the leather spokeshave should be further down on your list of purchases.

Various awls: the three on the right are round awls, and the others are diamond awls.

AWLS

Awls are indispensable when you are sewing leather, because the needles used for leather handwork are dull and are not suitable for piercing directly through leather.

The awl used on sleeked leather has a diamond-shaped blade cross section and is called a

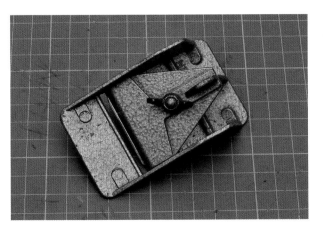

Schwertahle (sword awl) in German. It is used to prepierce the holds at an angle slightly oblique to the seam line. It is important to have a good haft that holds the awl securely, especially when you have to pull somewhat harder on it to get it out of the leather again. Hafts that have devices for changing the awl blades have not stood the test for me, since these usually do not hold properly in the fastener. A haft that has the awl blade driven in works better.

On the diamond awl blade, the tip is ground to a needle point at the factory, but the sides are left relatively rough. It is better to modify the awl slightly: grind the sides clean and polish them, then sharpen the tip to a millimeter so that it is semicircular and sharp. This way, you can influence the direction a bit more when piercing the holes, and due to the polished sides the awl slides into the leather more

TIP

When piercing the leather, you have to use two fingers to hold it from the other side. For your safety, you can also use a cork and stick the awl into the cork. Do this especially with workpieces that are hard to hold in a clamp.

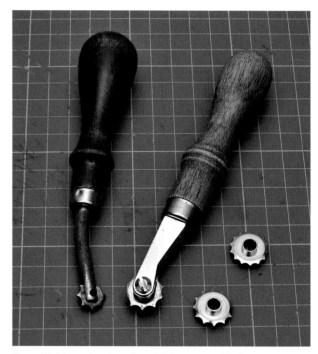

easily. Even if only the top third of the diamond awl is ground knife-sharp on the sides, this is enough for piercing the holes, while the lower part just widens the hole more. After a few minutes, the leather will take its initial shape again and forms itself closely around the thread. Finishing the edge especially will close the hole again.

Round awls work well either in chamois leather or to push the thread in the seam to the side when you are sewing the last two stitches.

The stitching wheel on the right comes with two interchangeable wheels with different stitch spacing.

STITCHING WHEEL (STITCHING INTERVAL MARKER)

To ensure that the individual holes for a seam are evenly spaced, you should first mark them with a stitching wheel. This tool has a star wheel, which presses the marking for the individual stitches into the leather. On most wheels, however, the hole spacing is too narrow and designed only for very thin leather. Either you then use only every second marking, or use a wing divider, which is something you should purchase anyway.

In order to ensure that you keep the individual holes for a seam at a regular interval, you should mark these beforehand, using a stitching wheel.

GLUE

You can also glue leather, but that is a science in itself. If you are using glue for an absorbent leather backing, this involves using a contact adhesive, which is applied to both the pieces to be glued and then has to be left to flash off. After a few minutes the glued surfaces can then be pressed and hammered together. The pressure applied during bonding is responsible for its later durability.

Adhesive for leather is available in various container sizes and from different manufacturers.

Two pairs of punch pliers and a drive punch (*left*).

DRIVE PUNCHES / PUNCH PLIERS

To punch leather cleanly, drive punches or punch pliers are indispensable. You should buy a pair of punch pliers from a leather tool specialty supplier. With punch pliers, you can punch holes that are only 1.2–1.6 inches (3–4 cm) from the edge; beyond that, 0.24 inches (6 mm) is the biggest diameter you can get. You can make any holes that are set farther from the edge only by using a drive punch. When you are buying drive punches, you should pay attention not only to the quality, but also to whether the tool has been polished to be as flat as possible. Otherwise, they might get stuck in the leather. Also, the wall thickness of many cheap drive punches is too thick,

which drives a "wedge" into the leather. If you are working with narrow hole diameters and thick leather, this can tear the grain side. Furthermore, they are hard to drive through the leather and make the hole wider in a way you cannot control, so that when you use a 0.16-inch (4 mm) drive punch, you get a 0.24-inch (6 mm) hole on the grain side. In such a case, you should fall back on using a borer that bores the hole properly.

> **TIP**
> You can also use a pair of revolving punch pliers like you do a drive punch to punch holes in places that you otherwise would not be able to reach with the pliers. To do this, turn the pliers around.

Two different, adjustable chamfer tools.

CHAMFER TOOL

To be able to fold or crease leather cleanly, you have to thin the inside of the fold first. To do this, there are special gouging tools that cut out a V-shaped or U-shaped notch in the leather, like a wood plane does. There are chamfer tools with adjustable cutting depth and fixed models. Such a tool is a luxury for your first attempts in leather crafting; you can also do this work by holding a knife at an angle. Another possibility is to work using a freehand-guided stitching groover.

To be able to fold or crease leather cleanly, you have to thin the inside of the fold first.

TIP

On thick leather, a hole punched with punch pliers is very conical in shape. You can widen this hole a little more, working from the flesh side, by using an offset punch that is one number smaller. This if often necessary when you are working with rivets and button studs.

Buckles

MATERIALS FOR BUCKLES

There are huge differences in quality among buckles, especially among belt buckles. The only materials you should consider should be brass or stainless steel. Galvanized or chrome-plated iron buckles lose their coating at some time and then look shabby. Brass buckles are given a patina, especially when they are used on horse harnesses.

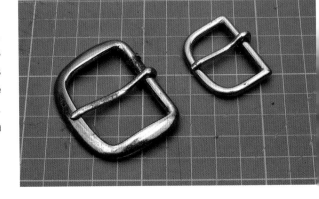

SIMPLE BUCKLES

The simplest form of a buckle is a piece of wire bent into a D-shape with a slightly bent tongue. There are also simple buckles that are nevertheless high quality; for these items, the material is either cast or cleanly made, while the tongue is round and lies neatly on the bar.

On inexpensive buckles, the end of the tongue that lies on the bar is simply hammered out wide and rolled, which makes it much wider than necessary. As a result, the slot in the belt must also be much wider than necessary, which weakens the belt unnecessarily. Using a 0.16-inch (4 mm) round piece of brass material, you can quickly bend a new, lovingly crafted tongue, which can be exchanged for the shoddy one. You can also carefully bend the existing tongue and then shape it by using a belt sander or file. Also pay attention to the tip, which usually has a burr that has been hammered wide. Here, you can improve the way it works significantly with some strokes of a file, which also protects the holes in the leather.

ROLLER BUCKLES

A simple buckle with a piece of metal over the bar is called a roller buckle. This roller protects the leather when you pull it through, and therefore such buckles are often attached to pack straps. Such small matters as using a roller buckle make the difference between lovingly crafted workmanship and mass production, where it is necessary to save a few cents in production. This has its revenge ultimately when the surface of the leather gets damaged by the sharp edges of the buckle.

DOUBLE-BAR BUCKLES

Double bar buckles are made with two bars. The tongue lies on one, and the free end of the belt is drawn through the other. These are found mainly on horse harnesses and are therefore available only in narrow sizes. But they also cut a fine figure on backpacks.

TIP It takes just as long to sew on a bad, inferior-quality buckle as it does for a slightly more expensive, high-quality buckle. You should not save on buckles, because it makes a difference.

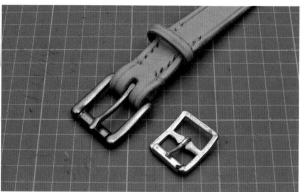

PLATE BUCKLES OR CONCHOS

These flat pieces, which are equipped with a bar for the end of the belt and a short tongue or hook for the holes in the belt, are called plate buckles or conchos. These are made mostly in the United States and are often significantly larger than a commercial buckle. On plate buckles, the design is in the forefront. These pieces, which are made of silver and elaborately decorated, are used at rodeos as winner's trophies.

Plate buckles the size of a beer glass coaster are not unusual. Of course, a high-quality belt belongs with such buckles.

On plate buckles, the design is in the forefront.

Fundamentals
Snap Fasteners and Rivets

MOUNTING SNAP FASTENERS

Snap fasteners have been used on leather goods only for a few decades. They come in two types: one type has a safety device that lets it be snapped open only on one side, and the other type is the models that work in any direction. You can attach the safety snap fasteners to belt loops, for example, without any worry, if you have made sure beforehand that they are properly aligned.

The bottom part is naturally set inside the workpiece and should therefore be masked with a thin piece of leather to protect the contents of the bag. Make sure that the leather is not too thick, so that it is still possible to splay the shank of the snap fastener cleanly. For thicker leather, there are bottoms with extra-long shafts. For even thicker leather of several layers—for example, on a holster for a heavy-duty revolver—drill a clean hole and screw down the back to the snap fastener fast.

For snap fasteners, it is important that the hole is the correct size. If in doubt, take a remnant piece of leather and punch a hole in it so that you can check the fit. Especially with soft or chamois leather, the snap fastener would rip out again if the hole were too big.

For snap fasteners, it is important that the hole be the right size. If in doubt, take a remnant piece of leather and punch a hole in it, so that you can check the fit.

BUTTON STUDS (A.K.A. BUTTON OR ROUND-HEAD RIVETS)

So-called button studs offer an elegant way to fasten bags; these are also called button or round-head rivets. As the German name (*Beiltaschenknopf* = hatchet sheath stud) suggests, they were particularly used for making hatchet sheaths. The bottom part of the button stud is screwed in; the thread is previously coated with Loctite or nail polish to prevent any unintentional loosening. Just one "buttonhole" is cut into the leather flap. But not just any kind; rather, one with a gimmick: there is a pull on the leather flap, in the direction in which it opens. At the end of the buttonhole you should punch a hole that matches the diameter of the shank of the button stud. Now cut a slit into the leather, against the pull,

so that the strap can be pushed over the stud. At the end of this slit, punch a very small hole so that the slit will not tear further. Use special care when making a slit in the belt, because if you have measured it incorrectly, it is difficult to repair. As an aid, you can first punch the hole for the button stud and then close the bag or the strap and trace the hole with an awl; of course, you do this on a bag that contains something. You can comfortably make the fastening quite taut at the beginning, because the leather stretches over time.

Use special care when making a slit in the belt, because if you have measured it incorrectly, it is difficult to repair.

SETTING RIVETS

On certain workpieces, a well-placed rivet can improve its durability. But this presupposes some things. The ready- made or hollow rivets made of sheet metal, which are used almost everywhere, are worthless. People are happy to use these on inexpensive knife sheaths to protect the lower seam at the tip, so that the blade does not cut through it. This testifies to a false design of the sheath and is cheap and shoddy work. The upper ends of the seam on bags, or the carrying straps on backpacks, are often reinforced with proper copper rivets because these have a wide head that distributes the pull over a larger area. Furthermore, the rivets are attached in such a way that the holes are punched out cleanly and the seam is not affected. To first lay down a seam and then to pierce through it with the rivets is the wrong way to work, but you can certainly use this to make a "repair."

A copper rivet consists of a rivet with an extra-large and flat head. The rivet is in principle substantially longer than the material to be riveted is thick. The side with the head is the "decorative end" and therefore is set on the visible side of the workpiece. Push the rivet through the previously bored or punched hole, and then put on the washer

Insert the rivet through both leather layers.

Fit on the washer.

The rivet setter has two holes; the smaller and deeper one is necessary to drive down the washer.

The rivet setter is used to drive the washer down onto the leather.

from the back side. Use rivets made either of aluminum or copper, because iron rusts and leaves stains. Use the rivet setter, which you slide over the rivet shaft, to drive the washer downward, and at the same time press the leather together. In most cases, the washer will already be fastened tightly, so that it remains in place and will not be pushed upward by the leather as it stretches again. Now shorten the rivet shaft with a pair of pliers; the length that remains should be about the same as the measurement of the shaft diameter. Now rivet the shaft by using a light hammer on a solid metal support to form it into a mushroom-shaped head. Under no circumstances should you use a heavy hammer to deliver a powerful blow to the rivet, since this would only bend it to the side and ruin the workpiece. The right method is to use many light strokes to drive the material in the desired direction.

To remove a rivet again, simply file away the riveted "mushroom" and strike the shaft out through the washer.

Use rivets made either of aluminum or copper, because iron rusts and leaves stains.

Use a pair of pliers to shorten the rivet shaft to 0.08–0.12 inches (2–3 mm) above the washer.

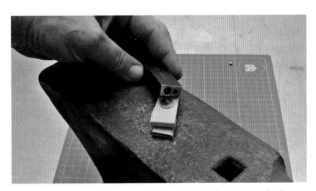

Set the rivet by using the head setter—the large, shallow hole.

Instead of using force, the process works better if you use some skill and a lot of light strokes to the edge of the rivet shaft, to form a mushroom shape.

Done.

Marking and
Cutting Out Leather

Use the cobbler's knife to cut it as much on the perpendicular as possible, so that the slanted part of the cut piece presses outward and the cut edge runs perpendicular to the "good" part of the leather.

MARKING LEATHER

To transfer a cutting pattern to leather, it is best to use a sheet of paper and a bone folder. Place the paper with the cutting pattern, not already cut out, on the grain side of the leather. Then use the bone folder to press the lines through onto the grain side of the leather, but not too hard—only so that you can

Use the bone folder to carefully press the lines of the cutting pattern into the grain side of the leather.

just see them. If you "draw it incorrectly," you can erase this line by using the back of the bone folder. Then you can cut out the cutting pattern from the paper. When making knife sheaths or holsters, it is especially important to check the shape once again before cutting the leather, so that you don't end up cutting out a left-handed holster when you are right-handed. If you have to mark the flesh side of the leather—which you should not use for marking if possible—it is best to use a soft 6B lead pen or ballpoint pen. Use a ballpoint pen only if you will not be able to see the lines afterward because they are covered over.

To cut inside curves cleanly, punch out the curve with a drive punch beforehand.

Then make the other cuts around the punched out circle.

On chamois leather, a soft pencil is likewise the method of choice, since it can be easily scraped off with a flat-held blade.

CUTTING OUT LEATHER

On chamois leather, you should cut using a heavy, sharp pair of scissors along the indicated line, because if you use a cutter or leather knife, you would stretch the soft leather when cutting it and the cutting pattern would no longer match the cut leather piece.

It is always best to cut sleeked or harness leather from the grain side and as much on the perpendicular as possible. A leather knife always has one straight side and one ground at an angle. When cutting, you should always hold the straight side along your marking and the side ground at an angle that is always outside the marking, in the direction of the cut piece. This way, you avoid making a slanting

edge, and if you make a slanted cut anyway, then the "excess" part is outside the pattern lines.

Incisions in leather (for example, to make belt loops for a sheath or holster) are first delimited using punch pliers, and then the slit is made up to the two holes. Always finish all cuts in leather with a punched hole, so they cannot tear further.

Narrow internal curves, for leather sheaths, for example, are first prepunched with a drive punch, and then the straight cuts are made around this circle. You do not have to strike the drive punch, just the larger caliber, with a hammer; it is enough to press it in by hand and then turn it, which cuts out the hole as if by itself.

Always finish all cuts in leather with a punched hole, so they cannot tear further.

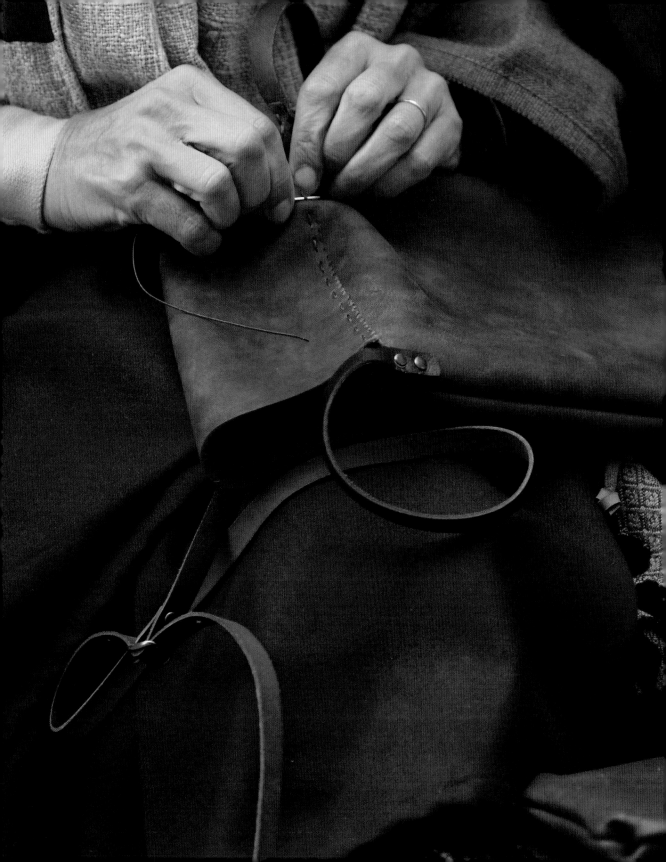

A Simple Seam

"If you want to learn to forge a sword, start with a fire poker."

Left: First you make a groove, and then the stitches are marked. First use the awl to pierce the leather and then sew with the thread. Then press in the decorative groove, and the edge is chamfered and polished.

Right: Two parallel seams are ideal; the right seam weakens the leather a great deal, and this is where the strap will tear.

WHAT MAKES A GOOD SEAM

There is a lot to consider about making a good seam. What is particularly amazing for many newcomers is the fact that a good seam holds as long as the leather itself. When sewing leather, there are several reference points and rules of thumb; if you take account of them, these help create a professional appearance for your work.

The distance of the seam from the edge should be one to one and a half times the simple leather thickness. If, for example, the leather for a knife sheath is 0.16 inches (4 mm) thick, then the seam should lie 0.16–0.24 inches (4–6 mm) away from the edge. The hole spacing for the seam should likewise be one to one and a half times the simple leather thickness, even if the edge might be 0.47 inches (12 mm) thick, because the leather has been doubled and you inserted some piping.

If you are sewing two leather straps together, the two pieces should overlap at least as much as double the leather width. It is not wrong to even make it three or four times the width of the strap; however, even more than this will not increase the security. Leather straps, which are to take up the pull, should always be sewn parallel to the pulling direction and never crossways. The stitches would only weaken the straps.

If the strap is so wide that a seam on both the right and left is insufficient, then you should sew a third seam, and if necessary another seam, in the middle of the strap and parallel to the lengthwise edges. Another possibility for sewing two straps

A good seam holds as long as the leather itself.

together is to design the seam along the length of the strap as a wavy line; this method will also not affect the tensile strength. This method is often used on belts that are made double with a second piece of leather.

A good seam is cleanly recessed, which protects the thread so that it does not fray or wear through. If two pieces of leather are to be sewn together, the ends of the leather should be thinned to half or one-third of the original leather thickness, and indeed to about the length of two stitches.

Another possibility would be to finish the end of the upper piece of leather to a pointed tip and then follow this line as you sew. These methods are often used on weapon belts, which are especially wide and are fastened with a sewn-on narrow buckle, but also on belt loops to hold knife sheaths or revolver holsters.

FASTENING THE LEATHER FOR SEWING

To be able to sew two or more pieces of leather together, you first have to fasten them so that the pieces cannot slip apart. Furthermore, you would like the work to come out so that all the pieces are still aligned as you make the last stitch. This is not a big problem for straight seams, but it certainly is a challenge if, for example, you are making a knife sheath from a piece of saddle leather folded over 0.16 inches (4 mm) thick with an inserted piping. These pieces are under tension and must also be

aligned and fastened in this position. Glue certainly works for fastening something lightly, but the pieces can still shift against each another and, in the worst case, also come loose from each other. Using glue is not sufficient, particularly on thin intermediate layers. There is nothing wrong with using glue on belt buckles, which are sewn fast by simply folding over the leather.

To fasten pieces of leather for sewing, nail them together carefully, using thin, not-too-short nails. Nails are almost like pins for a leather crafter. Before you begin, you should chamfer out the groove for the seam and mark the holes with the pricking (stitching) wheel.

To fasten pieces of leather for sewing, nail them together carefully, using thin, not-too-short nails.

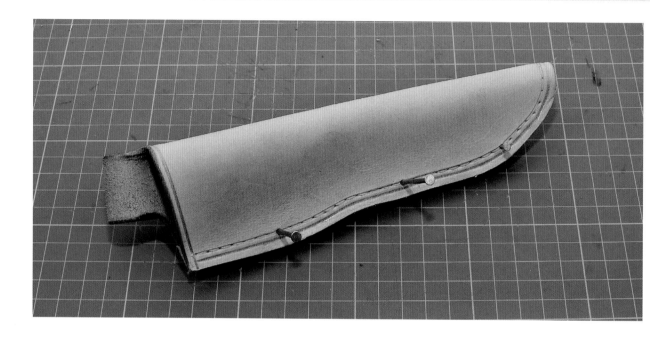

You should now carefully insert a nail at every five to ten stitches, so that it comes out the other side exactly at the designated place in the seam. For knife sheaths, it is advantageous to first insert a nail both at the upper and lower ends of the seam and then in the middle, and to fasten the two pieces together only in between at the end. The more tension there is on the leather pieces, the more nails you need. Leave the nails sticking in the leather until they get in your way as you sew, and then just pull them out and you can reuse them.

HOW TO PIERCE THE HOLES

Many beginners get into sewing leather from making knives and now want to make sheaths. As a result, they usually have a very well-equipped metal

Always pierce the holes with an awl.

workshop and have a drill press. What could be more obvious than to drill clean holes for the thread? Simply clamp in a fine, 0.06-inch (1.5 mm) drill and you can already get started. But the whole thing has a decisive disadvantage: the drill cuts material away and throws it out as chips, so that the hole is and remains 1.5 mm in diameter. It cannot close up again, and the round hole will always remain visible. In addition, the loss of material weakens the leather. Drilling may seem attractive at first, but it is the worst choice from a craftsman's point of view.

You should therefore always pierce the holes for sewing leather with an awl: for sleeked leather, use an awl with a diamond blade cross section, and use a round awl for chamois leather. On chamois leather, the latter tool will only displace the material but will not remove it, as punch pliers or a drill will do. On sleeked leather, the diamond awl doesn't remove any material. Due to the slightly slanting stitch, it also will not create a torn edge, which could weaken the material. In addition, the

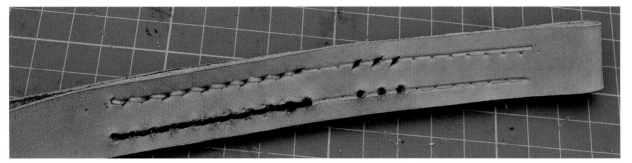

For comparison: in the image above, the top row shows the seam with the holes pierced with an awl; the bottom row shows holes drilled with a spiral drill and sewn with black thread—the aesthetic difference is great.

thread is drawn into one or another end of the stitch, and despite any uneven initial stitches, the seam appears relatively neat. As a result, with a little practice you can achieve pleasing results even as a beginner.

When piercing the holes, it is important to pierce them out by using your eye and skill, so that the awl comes out again in the seam groove on the other side of the leather. Even if the back side naturally does not look quite as beautiful as the visible front side, the thread should nevertheless come to lie in the groove, to protect it from wear.

SEWING

To sew a good and visually appealing seam, it is important to work as evenly as possible and always in the same way. For sewing, the workpiece is clamped in a lacing-stitching pony. At the beginning, you should sew long, straight pieces because they are easier to pull tight than short, curved seams are. The individual stitches are not arranged in a line, but slightly at an angle. This ensures that you will not create any torn edges.

The ideal angle for the path of the thread is, if you are looking at the seam from the front, from "two o'clock to eight o'clock." At the same time you should try to hit the seam groove on the other side. This can sometimes be easier on thick leather than on soft leather, since the latter likes to slide away while you sew. If you notice that you are shifting the seam, pull the awl back a bit, change the angle, and then pierce again, in the hope that you will now hit it.

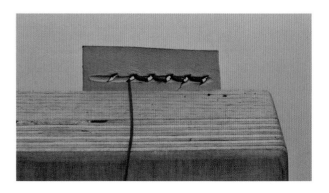

When you sew, as a rule you tend to make the motion from behind toward yourself. Furthermore, the first needle is always inserted from the back of the leather and then the needle [is drawn through][text missing] from the front. Always try to do this in the same way, so that the seam looks even after sewing.

Sewing also involves using an effective way of working, and as a result, the following method has crystallized out over the centuries: If you are right-handed, you grasp the awl with your right hand and do not lay it aside again during the whole process. You also hold a needle in this hand. You need to hold a needle only in your left hand. Then, use the awl to pierce through the leather from right to left, moving the awl slightly back and forth to widen the hole, and pull it out again. Next, stick the needle in your left hand through the hole from the back, as far as it will go. Now place the right needle under the left one at a right angle. Grasp both needles, turn your hand, and stick the right needle through the hole. At the same time, hold the awl in your right hand and use your left hand to pull the left thread downward in order to insert the right needle over the left thread. Try not to pierce the thread in the process, because then you cannot pull it tight later.

As soon as the right needle appears on the left, grasp it with your left hand and pull the thread through. Now grasp both threads—if necessary, grasp the thread a second time if it is too long—and draw both threads tight (and the seam as well) at the same time. Now you have a needle in your left hand and a needle and an awl (still) in your right hand. Pierce the next hole with the awl. At the same time, you can move the needle backward in your hand and pull the awl to the front, or you can work holding the awl in your "cupped hand." Over time, the process that is simpler for you will gradually crystallize out. Now stick the left needle through again and place the right one at a right angle under the left needle and pull it out. Now you have to sort the threads again, turn the two needles 90 degrees, and stick the right one through, pulling the threads through and pulling the stitch tight.

Use the awl to pierce a hole and then stitch through it immediately.

Right hand holds the awl and needle. Left hand holds the needle (if you are left-handed, the other way around, please!).

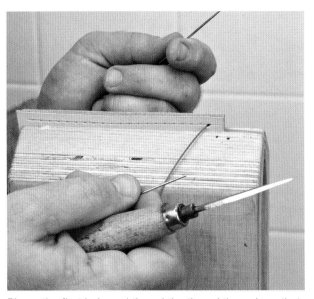

Pierce the first hole and thread the thread through so that it is the same length on both sides. Hold the awl and one needle in your right hand; hold just the second needle in your left hand.

Pierce the second hole.

The hole should be pointed from the top right to the bottom left.

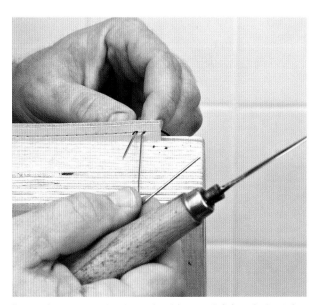

First stick the needle through with your left hand; the left needle is always stuck through first.

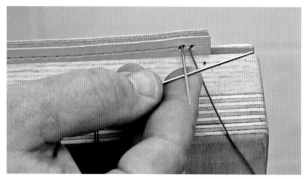

The left needle is inserted only as far as necessary until you can grasp it with your right hand. Now place the right needle under the left one at a right angle.

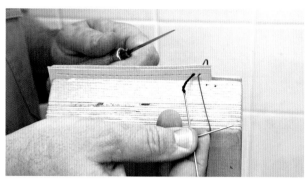

Grasp both needles between thumb and forefinger at the crossover point and draw the left needle completely through the hole. Do not pull the thread completely through the hole—you do this later.

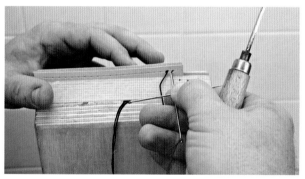

Now stick the right needle through while holding it above the left thread.

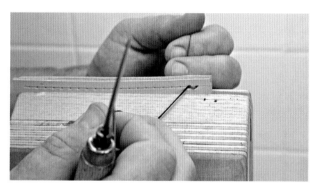

Now grasp the right needle with your left hand and carefully tighten both thread ends.

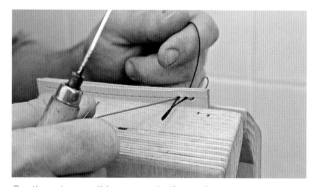

Continue to sew this way up to the end.

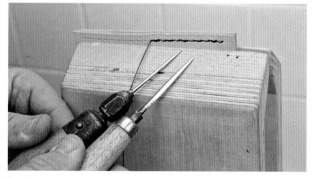

To finish the seam, switch to an awl with a round cross section.

Use the round awl to widen the first hole back along the way and stick the left needle through the hole first.

With the right needle still sticking in the hole, loop the left thread once around the needle so that you make a knot that comes to lie within the layer of leather.

You must pull this knot tight with special care.

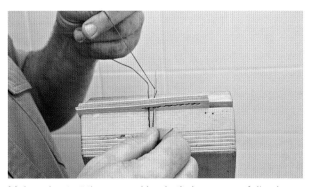

Make a knot at the second backstitch very carefully also, so that the seam is finished and will not come loose by itself.

Cut the thread ends off flush.

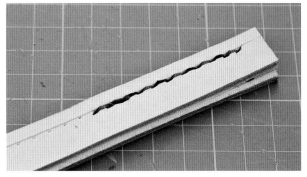

The seam is recessed into the previously chamfered groove.

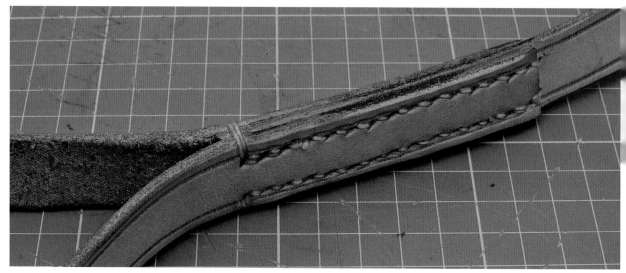

At this loop, pull the seam apart, so that the end is extra secure.

TRIMMING A SEAM

It is easy to start a seam—just draw the thread through and sew. But the end of a seam is always a challenge. Depending on the type of thread and the purpose of the workpiece in question, the end of the seam and way it is knotted will look different. If you are using synthetic thread, it is easiest to simply cut off the ends with 0.20 inches (5 mm) left over and fuse them with a lighter. If you are using waxed hemp thread, sew over the last two stitches once again. This naturally requires more space in the hole, so to do this, you should pierce a bigger hole with the diamond awl beforehand. If the holes are nevertheless too full after the first pass, you must use an awl again, to make more space. To do this, it is best to use a round awl, because a diamond awl would

Apply pine pitch to the thread again before making the last stitches.

damage the thread already in the hole. Before inserting the last stitches, you should rub the thread with pine pitch once again, since this makes it more adhesive. You should knot the last two stitches back by looping a thread once around the other, so that this simple knot is set in the leather after the thread is pulled tight. Cut off the protruding ends flush and work them into the seam by using the bone folder, so that they disappear from sight. If you are still unsure about how to use the bone folder, when back-stitching you can also end the seam in such a way that both ends are at the back side of the workpiece, and then knot them together.

On some seams—preferably when the two leather parts will be pulled apart—you can guide the two threads outward once again around the edge of the leather. Note, however, that the thread will fray quickly if you do not recess it in a groove, which should be carefully cut using a cobbler's knife.

BINDING THREADS

As discussed above, always keep the thread to just one arm span long. This also limits the length of the seam to 8 to 12 inches (20–30 cm). For longer seams, you might be tempted to cut off the thread and knot a new thread to it. This is exactly what you should not do, because you never know exactly where the knot will come to lie—in the worst case, it lies between the leather layers and makes them bulge out.

If you still have a relatively long end left over on both needles, so that you definitely could sew another belt loop, then work as follows: Knot the two ends together, and stick one needle through from the inside of the seam outward and stick the other needle through from the inside outward to the other side. Now the knot lies on top of and outside the two leather layers. This way, you can first sew back two stitches, as when starting with a new thread, and then sew on in the normal direction. Finally, cut off any knots that stick out.

When you are using up the last inch or two of thread, remember that the ends on the needle will get the most strain, and that is where the wax and pitch will be quickly rubbed off again. To have the thread hold securely at the end—and for the two backstitches—you should apply pitch and wax once again before making the last five stitches.

For long seams, such as on revolver holsters, sword sheaths, and the like, you should start your change to a fresh thread in good time, as soon as you realize that it will not be long enough. This is better than if you were to first insert another new thread at the last five stitches, and, as chance would have it, at exactly the point on the seam that has to bear the greatest stress.

To add on a new thread, finish sewing with the old thread by pulling the last stitch tight and knotting the two thread ends together over the edge of the leather. This allows you to trim the thread better later on. Insert the new thread into the old seam over two or three stitches and thus simply sew these two or three stitches double. Then, you can continue sewing completely normally. Finally, cut off the knot and the two thread ends flush.

Start the change to a fresh thread in good time!

The usual method is to "cobble on" more thread when sewing long seams. Avoid using a piece of thread that is too long, since it will lose all the more wax and pitch as you sew and will then no longer be as hard-wearing. A new thread is always the better solution.

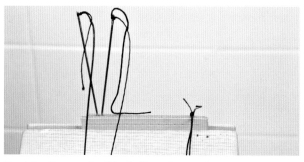

Knot the free ends of both threads together.

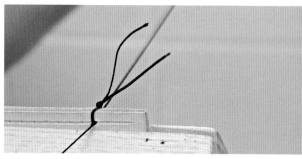

Start two stitches away from the end of the seam and pierce a hole. Guide the needles from both sides through the leather, so that the knot goes over the edge, where it will be cut off later.

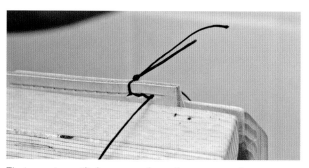

First sew two stitches away from the seam end.

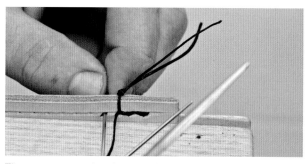

Then use a round awl to sew back over two stitches at the beginning and then continue with a diamond awl.

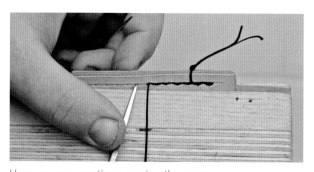

Here you can continue sewing the seam.

Finally, cut the knot off flush with the seam.

SEWING LEATHER STRAPS TOGETHER

Start by laying the two ends of the leather straps one atop the other and mark the overlap. In this area, you must not chamfer the edges yet, since these parts lie one atop the other and form a joint edge after they are sewn. Thin the respective flesh side of the leather strap ends to a leather thickness of 0.04 inches (1 mm), up to about 0.08 inches (2 mm) from the end.

Now draw on the seam, chamfer out the groove for the seam, and mark the stitching interval. Then tack both parts together with nails. Begin with the seam on one side and work your way to the end, then stitch two stitches back and cut off the thread flush.

Sew the seam exactly the same way on the other side, with the difference being that you use an attached thread here. To do this, knot the two ends of the thread and start two stitches from the end. Guide one needle from the left and the other from the right through the hole, so that the knot comes to lie on the edge of the leather. Then sew the two stitches to the end of one strap, then back again and up to the other end of the seam. From there, likewise sew two stitches back to secure the thread. Cut both thread ends and cut off the knot with the two ends. Use the bone folder or pricking wheel to make everything smooth, and finally make the seam equal.

You should attach two straps of the same thickness, with the grain side always on one side.

The leather stitches should be sewn at least to the length of three times the strap width.

The unprotected thread will later lie between the leather layers.

First sharpen the ends to a third of the leather thickness.

Make a groove to recess the seam and mark the stitches.

You can also tack the strap ends together, using nails, but it is simpler to use glue, as is done here.

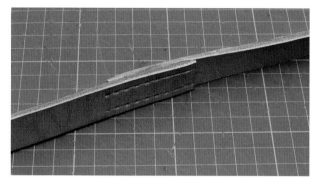

The ends are glued together to match and can now be sewn.

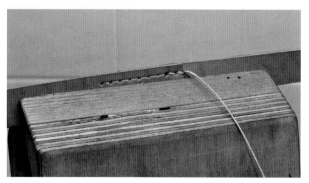

The first two stitches initially go backward to double the thread at this important place.

Then sew to the other end of the seam.

The last hole once again goes through only one layer of leather and should not be pierced too large.

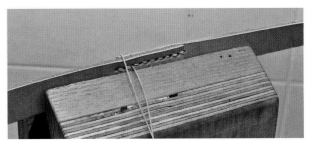

Sew two stitches back, cut the threads even, and turn the workpiece around.

To save thread, knot the two ends together and guide the thread over the edge.

First sew two stitches toward the right.

Then sew in the other direction.

At the end, again two stitches back

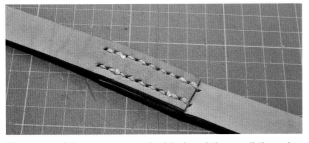

The ends of the seams are doubled and thus pull the edge of the straps downward to create a smooth transition.

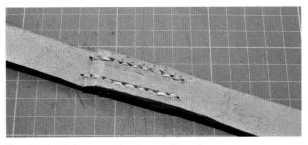

The back of the seam is also well made.

Projects

Sewing a Belt

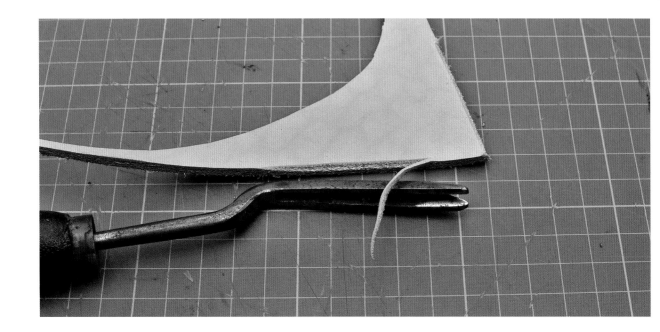

FINISHING AN EDGE

Let's start with something simple to illustrate the principle: a simple belt. You can buy the blanks for a belt ready made, and then you only have to pierce holes in one end, cut it to a point, and make a cut at the other end to attach the buckle tongue. Now just fold over the end and press in two snap fasteners, and the belt is finished. Unfortunately, it looks a bit strange and certainly is not at all sexy. A belt has a long edge; in fact, it consists only of edges, and if the leather belt blank is not finished any more, it will quickly get worn out when you wear it, so that it becomes even more unsightly than it already is.

It doesn't have to be that way: with a little skill, a leather edge can be easily finished so that it still looks attractive even after years of use:

First of all, press in a groove parallel to the edge, so that the leather turns slightly outward on the edge and the eye sees a finished border. Without this decorative groove, a leather strap is just a piece of unfinished leather. Then the leather edges are rounded off. This can be done either by using a sanding block and sandpaper, or with a tool called an edge beveler. As soon as the edge has been rounded off on both sides, it can be dyed either black or dark brown, or you can rub in an edge slicker, which makes the loose leather fibers adhere. In the industry they use mainly edge slickers or dyes, but hobby leather crafters instead make use of sandpaper, spit, and a bone folder.

On the flesh side—should this be visible—you can apply the decorative groove with a stitching groover.

If you have several layers of leather that are sewn together, finishing the edge is particularly important. Here, you should first cut the layers flush with a knife, especially if the piping protrudes from the bundle. Then sand the edge with a belt sander while changing direction at the same time, and finish your work with a 240 grain size sanding belt. Here, you should take care that not only the leather but also the grain side gets sanded, because this is easily turned over while you are sanding and remains in place as a thin skin. You don't see this skin at first because it is pressed onto the other leather layers, but at some point it will become unfastened again and then it looks very unattractive. You should first chamfer the edges after the edge surface has been sanded smooth. Wide edges look best when they are dyed with an edge dye.

If you have several layers of leather that are sewn together, finishing the edge is particularly important.

Press in a groove parallel to the edge, then chamfer the edges and dye them.

PLEASE NOTE

A piece of leather is finished only when the edge has been finished!

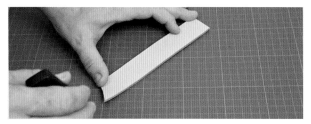

Place the leather firmly on a support and hold it fast with one hand.

Rub along the edge with the grooving tool and use it to press into the leather with light force at first, and then use more pressure and speed to make a decorative groove in the leather.

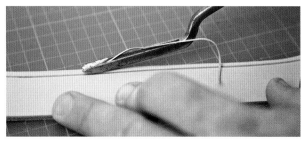

Use the edge beveler to cut a long strip away from the edge.

You should also see the edge on the flesh side of the leather.

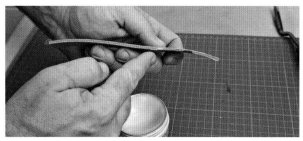

Use your fingers to apply leather grease or saddle soap to the edge.

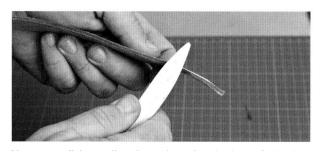

You can polish smaller pieces by using the bone folder in quick movements.

LEFT: A profiled wooden roller in a drilling machine helps for polishing the edge on larger pieces or long belts.

WHAT MAKES A GOOD BELT

As you have already seen in the previous chapter, a good belt is not just a piece of leather with a buckle, but rather it is a custom-made piece and provides decades of wear. When choosing the buckle, you should take note of how thick the leather is: the thicker the leather, the farther the interval from the bar to the front of the buckle must be, so that the leather will go through the buckle easily and it does not get "buckled" or bent.

The last hole in the belt should be as far away from the tip as is necessary so that you can still pass it easily through the buckle and slide it under the catch. Nothing looks more like something you have "grown out of" than a belt whose end you can just barely get through the buckle and that has many additional holes, like annual rings on a tree, all bearing witness to a growing beer belly. A belt should be much longer than necessary and have a lot of holes only if you are going to wear it over your clothes and hang weapons and tools from it. With this design, you can fasten it securely when wearing both summer and winter clothing. You can also punch holes all along the belt, so that it is possible to secure all your "stuff" from slipping off with leather straps. To do this, pass a strap each time from one hole to the other. This way, you can fasten on a knife sheath and other tools and pockets by a belt loop at the places you want them.

The thicker the leather, the larger the distance from the bar to the front of the buckle.

The last hole in the belt should be as far away from the tip as necessary, so that it can still go under the loop.

When choosing a color, keep in mind that the dark spots caused by your sweat show up especially on light-colored leather. As soon as these have become too apparent, make the strap darker.

TIP

The length of a belt is determined by the middle one of the five holes. From the tip of the belt, first go 4.7 to 5.9 inches (12–15 cm) back and set the first hole there. Then add the additional holes at a 1-inch (2.5 cm) interval. There is usually just a total of five holes in a trouser belt, so you can gain and lose weight and the belt always still fits. Now measure from the middle hole to the end with the buckle. Make sure that you do not measure to the center of the buckle, but to the point on the tongue where the middle hole will be hooked on. This can vary depending on the size of the buckle. Always pull the belt in such a way that the buckle lies in you left hand, and the free end with the holes in your right hand—buckles with designs are made exactly in this way. When you have placed the buckle exactly right on the leather, mark the bar of the buckle and the width of the tongue. For some buckles, you do not need to cut a slit for the tongue.

If the strap is too short to be folded over to fasten on the buckle, then use a matching piece of leather to make a doubled loop, which you sew to the belt from above and below. At the same time, it looks better if you don't sharpen the piece of leather too much and also don't sew it on flat, but rather design both ends in the same way as the belt tip and sew it on as a continuous piece. The seam running along the pointed tip does not weaken the belt.

To shorten a belt, don't cut off the tip, since this would shift the already frayed holes farther forward. Instead, cut off the buckle and shorten the strap at

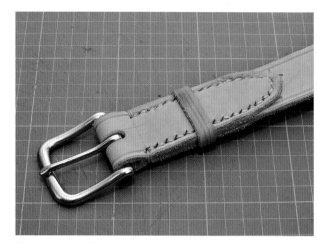

Here, a piece of leather was used to attach a buckle to a strap that is too short.

this end, and then sew the buckle on again. This method certainly takes more effort but looks much better.

The holes are often a weak point on industrially made belts or on your first self-made belts. You have to punch them cleanly, using a sharp drive punch so that the buckle tongue can pass straight through them, because the holes expand during wear and then quickly become too big. Making the holes with a nail or another pointed instrument is even worse. These first really start to fray and then tend to tear open. Holes look most professional when you use an oval drive punch to punch them out. The slot for the tongue should be cut neatly and not made too narrow, so it is easy to use the tongue. If the leather is particularly thick and the buckle is also thick, it may

Measure from the middle hole to the end of the tongue.

Holes look most professional when you use an oval drive punch to punch them out.

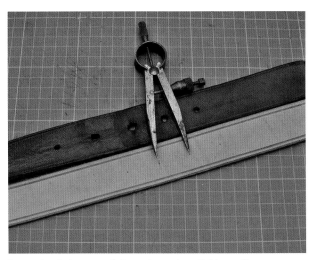

Draw the holes carefully, using wing dividers; if necessary, an old belt helps as a pattern.

Punch the holes with punch pliers with an oval drive punch.

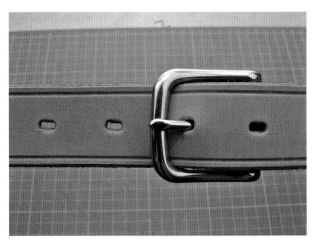

A slot gives more space for the tongue than a round hole.

For this thick leather, we inserted some piping in between.

> Before sewing it on, you should check once again whether the buckle has also been inserted correctly; I have already had to split some seams open again.
>
> **TIP**

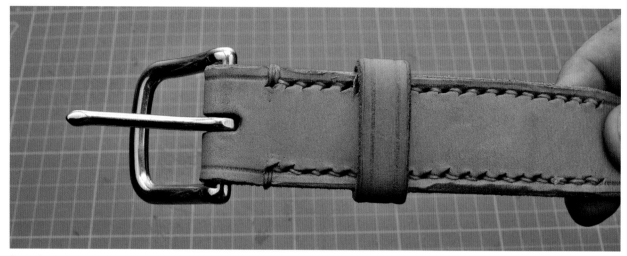

Sew the leather loop on at the same time. The best and most elegant solution.

be necessary to insert a piece of leather as piping in between, to compensate for the thickness of the bar.

On a trouser belt, there is no need to attach a loop for the free end of the belt. But it would not do any harm. The simplest method is to sew on a wire loop that matches the buckle. This will usually fit between two stitches and is easy to attach. The other option is to make a loop separately and then slide it onto the belt. It is even more elegant to sew the loop into the belt. For this, you should not make the loop too wide, so that you can use the awl to pierce once from the right and once from the left. This sewn loop does not have to hold too firmly and should therefore be made very thin, especially at the part that is sewn on, so that it does not make the belt too thick. This loop should be set in front of the first belt loop on the trousers. For a belt worn over your clothing, two loops won't hurt, but they should not be sewn fast, so you can move them.

A belt for normal suit trousers can be made of relatively thin leather, since this is usually sufficient and looks more elegant. But if you intend to wear a knife or a handgun on the belt, you will need thicker leather that is stable enough to prevent the edges from curling. Normal jeans are intended to be worn with leather belts of about 2 inches (50 mm) wide. The same is true of the belt loops on commercial holsters. With such a combination, the holster will sit perfectly and does not wobble. Furthermore, you can draw and reholster the weapon safely.

Belts made of double-layered leather are customary only if you are sewing some inexpensive, thick-split leather together with some thin leather. Otherwise, belts were made double only if you wanted to use the space inside as a secret hiding place for coins.

There are different ways to attach a buckle.

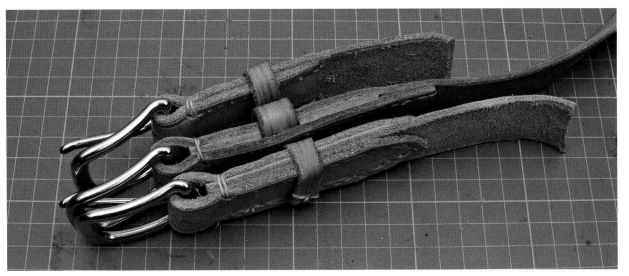

Three different ways to sew on a buckle. *Top*: simply folded over. *Middle*: folded over with an inside layer. *Bottom*: For a belt that is too short, sew it on with a separate piece of leather.

SEWING ON A BUCKLE

It is up to you whether you sew a buckle onto a simple folded strap or sew a separate piece of leather on from the front. For example, if you are working on a thin pack strap, you can also omit the seam completely and just use two rivets. If you want to sew, your work will normally be limited to making two parallel seams lengthwise along the belt. Avoid sewing crosswise on the belt, because that weakens the leather.

For a strap that is folded over, sharpen the piece of leather at the end, the length of two stitches, to about half the leather thickness. Care should be taken here when recessing the seam so that you do not accidentally cut through the leather with the stitching groover.

You should first press in the decorative groove, then make the recessed seam and finally chamfer the edges. If you were to chamfer the edges first, you would cut off the clean edge where you apply the stitching groover and the grooving tool.

Cut out the recess for the buckle tongue and chamfer the edges on the inside of the folded-over area.

When sewing, start at the most distant point, where the turned-over end of the belt stops. The first stitch goes only through the plain leather, and at the same time you should not push the awl completely through the leather—it is sufficient if the needle can pass through. Then pierce the second hole, but this time through the thinned part of the leather. When you pull the thread tight, you should do it carefully

> **TIP**
>
> You should be very conservative when greasing and oiling a belt, so that you don't stain your clothing.

so that you do not damage the thin leather. You can also start with a third hole and first sew two stitches back. This double seam, however, is hard to recess in the thinned leather.

From this point, you can set the stitches normally until you get to the last stitch before the buckle. Now, for straps on which there may be sideways pull that can affect the seam, the thread is guided outward once around the two leather layers. To do this, pierce the hole again especially large, and then sew as before, once from both sides. Now the thread lies on the right and left sides. Take the right thread, place it atop the workpiece on the left side, and stick it through the hole again from the left, but let the thread come out going upward between the two leather layers. Likewise, place the left thread on the right side and then stick the needle into the hole from the right, so that it also comes out in the middle. You should subsequently guide the thread twice over the edge of the strap.

To continue sewing, guide both needles between the leather layers to the other side and turn the workpiece on the stitching pony. Now pierce the first hole on the side of the buckle and guide the two needles outward on both sides. Move one thread to the other side and stick the needles through completely, as when making a normal stitch. Now you can finish the rest of the seam until you have arrived at the end. You can make the last stitch, on the thinned part, only with a needle, because it is not possible to recess as much thread there. From here on, sew back two stitches, while widening the holes with a round awl. Be careful not to pierce through the thread of the previous seam. After making the two backstitches, cut the threads flush. To make the work neat, you can roll over the seam once more with the stitching wheel that you used to mark the seam.

On straps that also have to withstand a sideways pull, guide the thread outside around the leather layers.

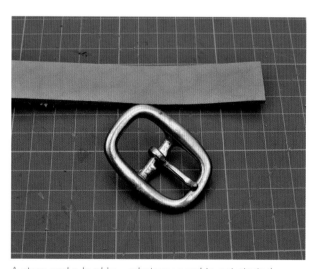

A strap and a buckle—what you need to get started.

Cut some piping and press a groove in the leather.

Thin the end of the leather to one-third of the original thickness.

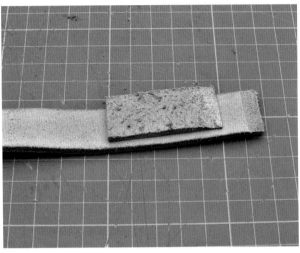

The piece of piping is also thinned but is made longer and even thinner.

Draw on the slot for the tongue.

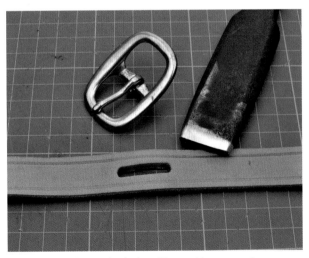

You can punch out the hole with an oblong punch; otherwise, punch two round holes with the punch pliers and cut out the piece between them.

Draw the seam and recess it right away.

Use a stitching wheel to mark the interval between the stitches.

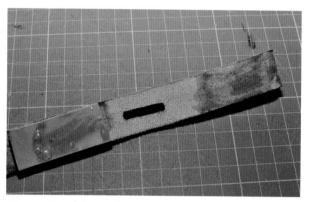

Glue on the piping and pass the strap around the buckle so that you can sew it.

The design viewed from the side.

For sewing, clamp the strap in the stitching pony.

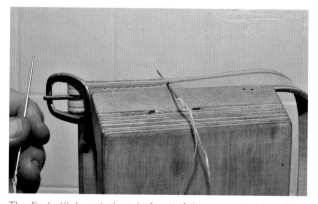

The first stitch, set close in front of the second piece of leather, goes through only one layer.

To guide the thread to the other side, stick the needles in the middle, going outward.

Pull the two loops tightly around the outer sides of the leather and guide the needles downward.

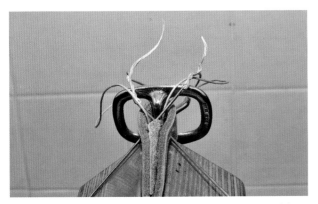

The piece is clamped; guide the needles from the inside outward.

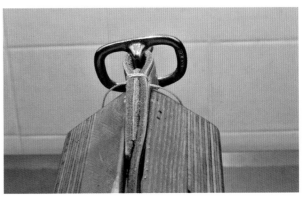

Sew once over the edge of the leather, then continue toward the end.

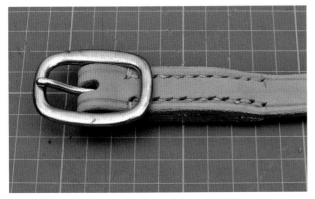

The finished seam is a perfect piece of handiwork and durable.

The finished belt with sewn-on buckle.

SETTING A RIVET FOR A PACK STRAP

Simple pack straps can also be made quickly and easily with one or two proper rivets.

On a regular pack strap, which you use to fasten your equipment to your backpack, you can find many small special features that would also be interesting for other projects, such as for a dog collar, but these mostly fall victim to the manufacturer's efforts to cut costs. On the one hand, you can attach so-called roller buckles on pack straps. These have a tube for a roller on a cross brace, so that the strap can be pulled tight with little friction. On the other hand, a pack strap usually has a double buckle, which is shaped like an eight, and which you can use to draw the free end of the strap right through the second part of the buckle. A loop is often attached to the strap so that the rest of the free end can also be fastened so it doesn't stick out and flap around. The holes are set close together to ensure a very fine adjustment; this ideally lets you adjust the pressure on the materials you will fasten on with the strap. Third, a pack strap should be long enough to allow you to easily roll up even the thickest piece of clothing tightly, because there is still enough length left on the free end so that you can grasp it with your hand.

For example, if you use straps with roller buckles on an animal, its hair can get caught in the buckle. Therefore, you must first sew a piece of leather underneath that extends sideways as far as necessary to prevent you from tearing out any hair when you pull the strap tight.

Narrow pack straps with a double-roller buckle and a loop made of sheet metal can also easily be held together with just two rivets.

Cut out the hole for the tip of the buckle tongue and align the buckle on the strap.

Once everything fits, use an awl to pierce a hole through both leather layers, exactly at the place where the rivet will be set later.

The matching rivet with washers and a combination tool made of a rivet setter and nail puller

Make a hole through the previously marked spots on the leather.

Then push the rivet through the two leather layers and fasten the washer on the rivet. This can be pushed onto the rivet shaft only with force, which is also what you want.

Use the rivet setter to drive the washer as far into the leather layers so that they are lightly pushed together. However, work cautiously so as not to damage the leather.

Pinch off the protruding part of the rivet shaft so that 0.08–0.12 inches (2–3 mm) remain.

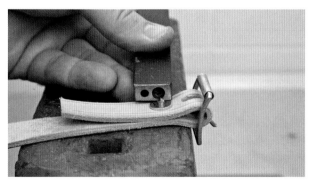

Use the nail puller to form the rivet shaft into a mushroom shape, so that the washer can't slip off.

The best method is to use a lot of light strokes and a light hammer, which forms the rivet into a mushroom shape. By no means should you try to ram the rivet through by using a heavy hammer and heavy strokes.

Sewing a Dog Leash

After making a belt, a dog leash is an interesting but simple practice piece.

A handsome dog leash made of real leather, well handcrafted, is just the proper formal outfit for your dog at the dog show or at the *Hubertusmesse* — the German mass celebrating St. Hubertus, the patron saint of dogs.

A custom-made leash does not need any buckles to adjust it, and this way you eliminate corner edges on which our friends could get caught, or that make a clatter. You could also eliminate all the buckles and sliders that are used on a bought leash to makes sure that it works for every customer and every dog. It is best to take the measurements from another leash that you have already adjusted to the right size. Or you can make a pattern by using a piece of package cord. Think about it: as you take the measurements in your apartment, consider that the leash also has to fit over thicker clothes in winter. If you have been able to get a continuous strap, then this is very helpful, since otherwise you have to patch on a piece of leash to the loop to go around your body. The continuous straps are usually glued together several times, which, however, is done so well that you can see only if you look closely. Try in any case to use a single strap, which certainly should be sufficient for a simple dog lead. You can either make the collar separately or attach it at the same time. It is also possible to incorporate a coupler so that you can walk two dogs at the same time.

The attachable leash used for hunting is usually made with a "limited slip" or "choker" collar, which is simply pulled over the dog's head. A

You can either make the collar separately or attach it at the same time.

built-in stop prevents the dog from choking himself too much. To this extent, the term "choker" is also incorrect, but it has entered everyday language.

The "limited slip" is adjusted so that it indeed encircles the dog's neck when pulled tight, but naturally does not compress it. You should be able to easily get your fingers between collar and neck. The open position is adjusted so that you can only just pull the collar over the dog's head. At this adjustment, it is hard for the dog to weasel his way backward out of the collar.

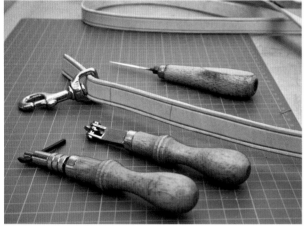

Draw the seam, chamfer out the groove for the seam with the stitching groover, and mark the stitches.

Thin down the free end, using a cobbler's knife.

Here it is enough to cut away one-third of the leather thickness over a few millimeters; you are just trying create a smooth transition.

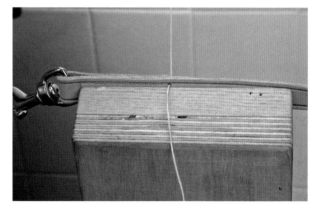

The first hole should be placed in front of the second leather layer and thus lead only through the long end. Pull the thread through the hole so that both ends are the same length.

The next hole then goes through both leather layers.

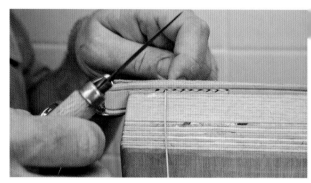

Now sew on the carabiner.

The last hole has to be pierced a little bigger, since here the thread goes through twice.

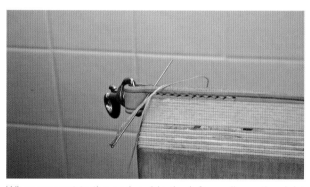

When you get to the end, guide the left needle on the right side and insert it so that the needle points between the two leather layers.

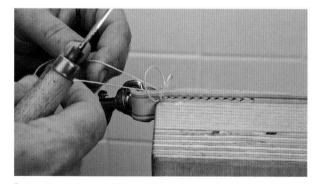

Guide the right needle over the edge of the leather and stick it through from the left side, so that this needle also appears between the leather layers. Then pull carefully.

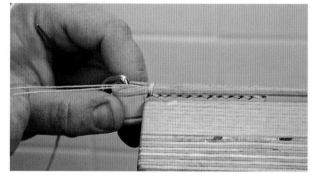

The two threads each go over the edge and thus absorb the sideways pull.

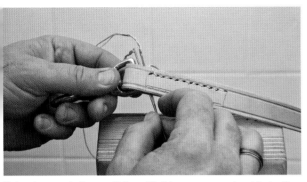

Take the workpiece off the stitching pony and guide both needles to the other side.

Clamp the workpiece for the second part of the seam, with the carabiner in, and pierce the first hole again to make it somewhat larger.

Insert both needles between the leather layers so that they point outward, and pull the threads tight.

Guide the two threads once over the edge and insert the needles from left and right through both leather layers.

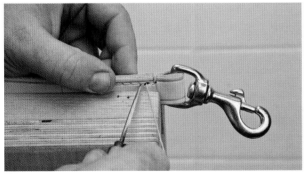

From now on you can sew completely normally. Now there should be two threads lying over this edge.

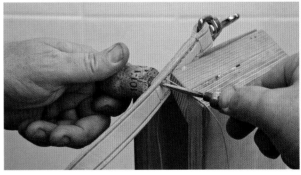

If you cannot clamp the last end the right way, then stick through the leather into a cork. Finish the seam by going two stitches back.

You could attach the collar directly to the leash and make it from one piece, but it is always better to integrate a stable swivel between the leash and collar. Here it is also possible for you to make the collar out of some much-broader leather or to line it with thin leather. Sew in a ring to make a stop and a second one to make a slide, and possibly a third one at the end, if this is not sewn directly to the swivel. Try to get a squared ring to use as the slider, because it will not ruin the shape of the leather. The disadvantage of a round slider is that it will abrade the leather along its length and rub it on the edges.

You can make a simple collar with a buckle by attaching a D-ring to hook into the leash carabiner. Usually these are sewn on the collar at the top, but it makes much more sense to push this D-ring onto the collar and fasten it with a band of leather. The pull from the ring does not then go onto the seam and the leather, but only on the collar itself. The leather band is only for fixing the position of the ring. Place the buckle as far from this D-ring so that the end of the collar can still be pushed under a catch. Depending on the circumference of the dog's neck, try to place the buckle as far up as possible on the loop, which is more convenient when you are putting the dog on the leash. The carabiner at the end of the leash should be of decent quality. When a strong, male wire-haired pointer starts jumping when he is on the leash, a cheap carabiner made of die-cast zinc will quickly give up the ghost and release the dog, who then will do something like run across the heavily traveled road when chasing a cat and could be run over. Good carabiners made of stainless steel are available from sailing suppliers. Simply buy a size larger, because it is easier to use them when you are wearing gloves in cold weather. Scissor snap hook carabiners will release under pressure and let the dog immediately run free. Swivel-eye snap hook carabiners will indeed open under pressure, but the dog is not immediately let free; however, you have to check him often.

FINISHING THE DOG LEASH

The middle seam is made up of the loop for your body and the actual leash. Here you sew three layers of leather together.

A larger carabiner is easy to use when wearing gloves during the winter.

Start with the simple leash and stick the next hole through all three layers.

At the end, where the loop for your body starts, sew over the edge once and then back two stitches. You have to start with a new thread on the other side: there is unfortunately no easy solution for getting the thread over to the other side.

Sewing a Belt Bag

A belt bag is just the right project for practicing how to use your fingers or if you want to learn how to sew. You do not use a lot of leather, the sewing is not difficult, and, besides, such a belt bag is practical. You should not choose a belt bag that is too small, so that you will have enough space to use your awl and needle on your first try. The bag should be able to hold a small, watertight tin canister or a box of small-caliber ammunition, which is how to determine its interior size. The back part of the bag folds over in one piece to make the cover and can also form the front side at the same time. To do this, just sew a piece of leather onto the sides, both right and left. Another possibility is to also sew the front side onto the back right side from one piece: Make notches under the corners in the front side to make them bend inward. It is necessary to first punch a hole with a drive punch in the middle of this cut, or it will not fold properly. Leave the sides of the front part long enough so that you can adjust these better after cutting out the pieces. Make grooves for the fold lines inside on the flesh side, so that they will come out more easily and cleanly.

There are three possible versions for making the belt loop: The first, simplest, and least attractive option is to make two slits in the back of the bag. The second possibility is to sew a wide strap on flat. To do this, you should insert a piece of leather, as wide as the belt, beneath the upper seam so that the belt does not fray the seam. This is quick and uncomplicated to do. The most elegant and final option is to wrap the upper part around the loop, so that the belt goes through this loop. In this case, however, the bag is held somewhat off the belt; it almost hangs in the loop. However, this version will hold up for an especially long time, and the loop can also be attached higher up on the bag. The bag therefore hangs lower overall on the belt, which makes it more comfortable to wear.

A belt bag is just the right project for practicing using your fingers or if you want to learn how to sew.

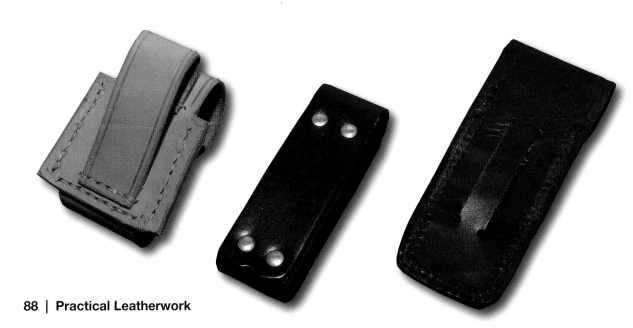

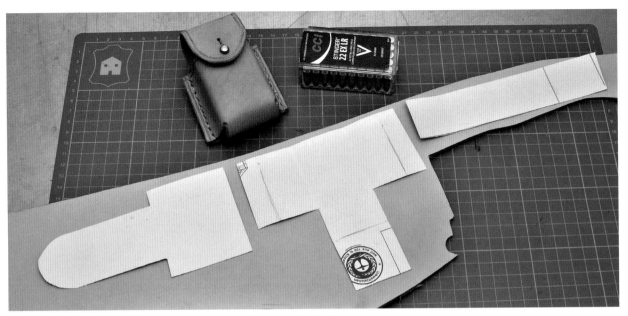

Place the templates with enough space around them on the leather.

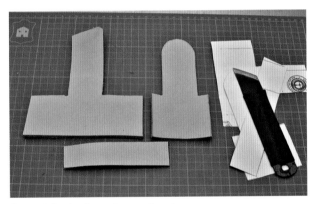

Cut out the leather pieces cleanly.

Before you sew, polish the edges, which will be hard for you to get at later on.

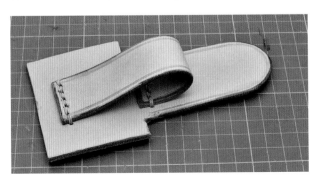

First sew on the belt loop.

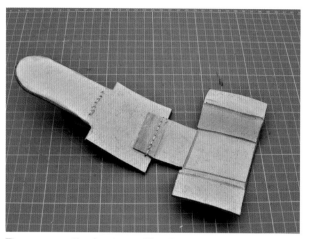

Then sew on the front part. The dents, which serve to make it easier to bend the leather, can be clearly seen here.

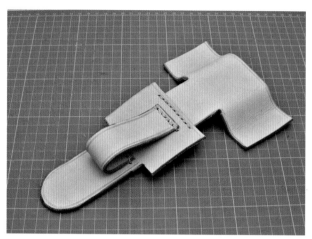

The sides for the front part are longer than necessary, so that it will be easier to clamp the workpiece better there.

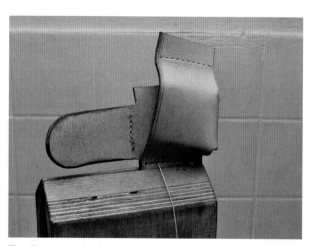

The first seam is done.

The second side is sewn the same way.

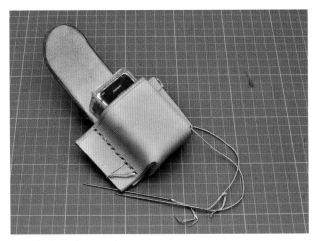

First fitting after sewing

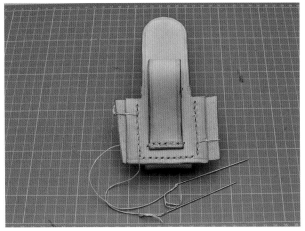

The bag viewed from the back: the too-long front parts can be seen very nicely; these are cut off flush when you trim the seam.

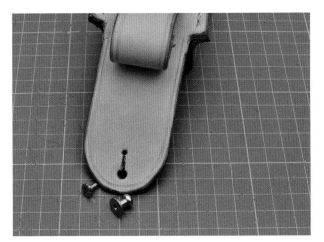

Mount the button stud.

The finished bag.

Sewing a Knife Sheath

SEWING A QUIVER-STYLE SHEATH

A custom-fitting knife sheath, made as a quiver-style sheath, is a work of art and may look trivial, something it certainly is not. You can do a lot of things the wrong way. In principle, a sheath should protect the knife itself, and the knife wearer from the knife. Furthermore, the scabbard should be comfortable to wear on your belt and not be a nuisance, and it should be easy to draw the knife and resheathe it, but it should also be fastened tight so that it "can't get lost." In fact, not all these things work together, but thanks to the special properties of leather, they still can be realized. To date, it has not yet been possible to design a sheath made of cheap plastic that combines all these qualities like a good leather sheath does.

When making a quiver-style sheath, it is an advantage to have a knife with a handguard that is either small or not there at all. Curved blades or knives with wide tips and tapered blades are particularly hard to sheathe. Knives with a distinct handguard are in good hands in a sheath with a safety strap.

A quiver-style sheath is made out of a single piece of leather, which is wrapped around the knife and sewn. In Scandinavia, these sheaths are made out of relatively thin leather, given a wood or synthetic application, and sewn on the back side. This is a special item and requires more than beginners' skill. The usual quiver-style sheaths are folded over the back of the blade and sewn along the cutting-edge side. At the same time, they cover around two-thirds of the handle. It is important to make sure in the design that the knife does not rest on its tip, but with the handguard to the inside, on a countersupport on the piping. Properly crafted, the knife snaps right in when you push it past the point of resistance ("dead point" in German) and the leather sheath, after it widens initially due to the oversized knife, returns to its original shape.

A quiver-style sheath is made out of a single piece of leather, which is wrapped around the knife and sewn.

To measure, you should first blunt the knife by putting an adhesive strip over the blade. Then you need packing paper or a hanging file folder, since DIN A 4 copy paper is too flexible and usually too small. Cut a sufficiently large piece out of the paper and fold it in the middle. Then, unfold the paper and place the knife with the blade back on the crease and lay it flat. Now fold the handguard at the lower end of the knife in the right angle toward the top. These two lines—the crease and the fold between the handguard and the blade—serve for guidance. With the knife in this position, trace the outline of the knife onto the lower side of the paper. Draw another line about 0.3–0.4 inches (8–10 mm) away from this line, this is the inside of the piping. Then comes a line of the thickness of the piping, also around 0.3–0.4 inches (8–10 mm). The tip should have at least 0.4 inches (10 mm) of space below it, so that it does not lie against the piping and cannot come close to the seam.

To measure, you should first blunt the knife by putting an adhesive strip along the edge.

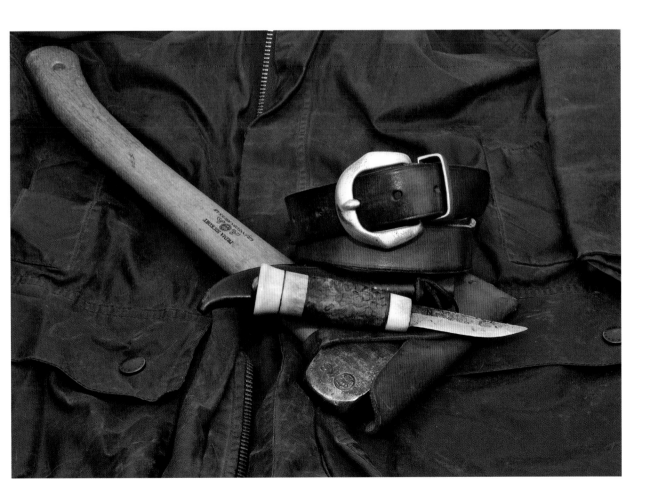

The design for the upper part of the sheath, which encloses the handle, depends on the shape of the handle. The piping should be shaped in such a way that the front part of the handguard can lie on it—be it ever so small. If the handle is particularly bulky, it is advisable to use another piece of leather as an intermediate layer. This keeps the opening of the sheath open, and the knife is not clamped in and stressed. It is important to create a slight arch in the piping, so that you have to use pressure to insert the handguard in the sheath; when it has been pushed past the point of resistance, it is again loosely held in the sheath. This is actually the ideal way you want it to be, but you will achieve this only when you take account of the characteristics of leather. The stiffer and more rigid the leather, the more difficult it is to create this condition. If the leather is softer and smoother, you can achieve a good and secure fit by shaping the leather when it is wet. However, if the fit is too loose, you can still use a tuck to rescue the sheath, provided that the piping is made wide enough.

It is ideal when you can shake the sheath with the knife inside it without the knife falling out. If you hold the sheath tight and move the knife, it should either not move at all or move up and down between the layer and the resistance point by just 0.04 inch (1 mm).

It is ideal when you can shake the sheath with the knife inside without the knife falling out.

Fold a sheet of paper and lay the knife on the edge of the fold and then draw on the leather sheath.

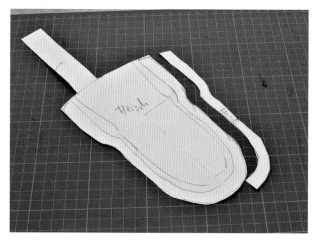

The cutout template and the piping next to it.

TIP Sewing on a separate belt loop saves a lot of material and waste.

Place the template on the leather and trace it.

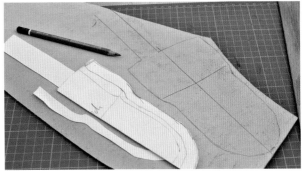

Also draw in the line between the handle and the blade and the fold line.

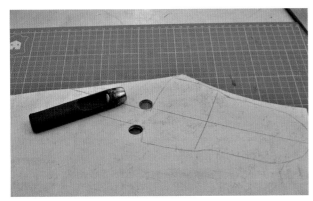

Punch out the clean transitions to the belt loop with a drive punch.

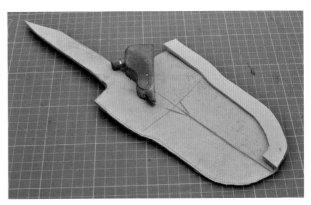

Chamfer out the fold line, using a grooving tool, so that it can be folded more easily.

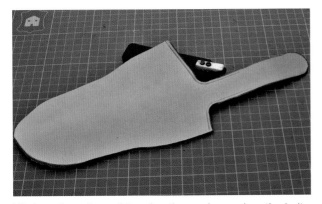

Work on the edges of the sheath opening and on the belt loop, because these places are hard to get at after the sheath is sewn together.

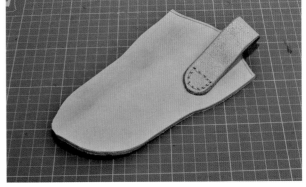

The neatly sewn belt loop.

Press a decorative groove into the sheath, chamfer the recess for the seam, and mark the stitches.

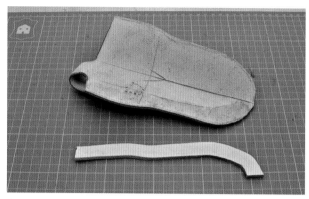

Coat one side of the sheath and the piping with glue and allow it to flash off slightly before gluing.

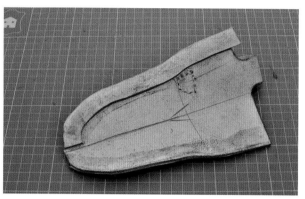

If the piping is glued on one side, also coat the other sides with glue.

Press the sheath together; it is fine if the piping shows a bit, and try it on for the first time.

Before sewing, you can also use a few nails to tack the file together.

Sew the sheath together, starting from the opening.

At the end, sew back over two stitches, widening the holes with a round awl.

The seam is finished.

Cut off the threads flush, then nothing will come undone.

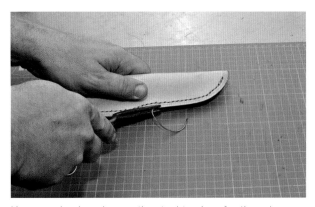

Use an edge beveler or other tool to chamfer the edge.

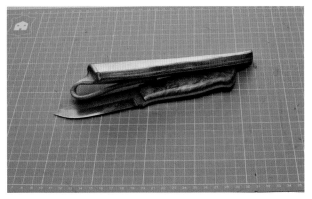

After sanding and polishing, the edge is clean.

Grease the sheath with a good leather grease. It works better using your fingers than using a rag or brush.

SHEATH FOR A BOWIE KNIFE

It is relatively easy to make a sheath for a Bowie knife, because here the fit does not matter. As long as the blade matches to the sheath, you can accomplish the rest quickly. The knife is simply fastened in with a safety strap over the handguard. At the same time, it is an advantage if the strap goes from the blade back side, because then the strap will not inadvertently be in the way and get cut when you put the knife back in the sheath.

For short blades and heavy knife handles, as well as very soft leather—as was formerly to be seen on most sheath knives, an additional strap is attached at the upper third of the handle. However, this does not serve to secure the knife very well but, rather, was incorporated because the handle can make the knife tip over, and soft leather cannot prevent this. If you are making a sheath yourself, you can easily prevent this from happening by sewing the belt loop on a little lower than is usual, which stabilizes the sheath.

The lower part of the sheath can be made out of either two parts, which are simply sewn together, or a single piece, which is folded over at the knife back. The upper part may also be made out of a single piece, which is simply folded over to form the belt loop. The other option is to sew a belt loop on separately, in which case you can determine the level where the sheath hangs on the belt.

If the knives are too large—starting from a blade length of about 10 inches (25 cm)—the knife will be too heavy and unwieldy, so that wearing it on your belt creates only drawbacks. Either you convert the sheath so that the knife is stuck on your belt on the left side, slanted from front to back, or you make the sheath so that you can fasten it to your backpack.

A knife sheath can be worn much more comfortably if you add on an additional belt loop for it, which is attached to the actual sheath by a ring. This is the solution that the Americans call a "dangler," which ensures that the sheath can tilt to

The knife is simply fastened with a safety strap over the handguard.

The lower part of the sheath could be made either in two parts, which are simply sewn one atop the other, or a single piece that is folded over along the back of the knife.

the side as you sit down, and does not push the belt upward.

How High Should a Belt Sheath Sit on the Belt?

This depends on how long the sheath is. A knife with a blade length of 6 inches (15 cm)—which is already very long for a hunting knife—and with a belt loop at the upper end of the sheath is very uncomfortable to wear. Each time you sit down, the sheath pushes upward and you have to somehow push the knife to the side. This is very annoying. Especially when the leather is stiff, there is no room for the sheath between your own butt and the chair. Here it is a good idea to use a separately sewn-on belt loop to raise the sheath so far upward that the tip will no longer hit the chair. It goes without saying that you have to twist yourself around quite a bit to draw the knife. So either use a shorter blade or take the Swedish way: Nordic knives with the appropriate

knife sheaths have a belt loop made of a very flexible leather strap. This lets the sheath dodge around in all directions and also move around on the belt. Furthermore, such a sheath has a tip like those on the long-toed medieval poulaine shoes, which ensures that the sheath slips to the side as soon as you sit down.

A knife sheath can be worn much more comfortably if you add on an additional belt loop for it, which is attached to the actual sheath by a ring.

Sewing a Leather Holster

WHAT REALLY MATTERS

Sewing a holster out of leather can be either a simple task or a very difficult one, depending each time on what you expect from the holster. Its main task, of course, is to hold the weapon securely and fast, and to protect it. On the other hand, it should also allow you to draw the weapon quickly and fluidly. To hold the weapon securely and protect it means a lot of leather and a simple design. The faster you want to draw, the less leather you should use. However, this also makes it more difficult to design the small amount of leather in such a way that the weapon is still secure and is protected to some extent. Usually, leather reaches its limits, and materials such as metal or Kydex are used.

A classic fast-draw holster for daily use.

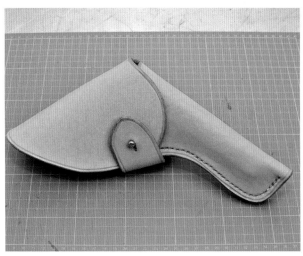

A modern fast-draw holster for concealed carry: this is where leather reaches its limits.

A classic holster for maximum protection of the weapon.

As an example for manufacturing a holster, here we are making a full-flap holster for a small, single-action revolver. This involves a relatively simple cut with a fit that is easy to produce. The cover closes with a button stud. Such holsters were already common in the time of front-loading revolvers, to protect the black powder from the effects of weather. They are often worn over your clothing because it is impossible to fold back the cover under your clothing. When it is worn on a belt, a right-handed person can wear it both to the back on the right, in front of the kidney, as well as on the left side, with the handle forward, on the front of the body. A holster on the left does not interfere with sitting in the saddle and is therefore known as a cavalry holster. Depending on how you wear it, the belt loop has to be arranged differently, since revolvers are generally equipped with longer barrels, and thus having a holster positioned in the right direction at an angle helps enormously for drawing. Since I am already wearing a knife on the back right half of my belt, the front left side offers itself, especially since it makes it easier for you to sit with your weapon in the holster. Another advantage for wearing it on the left side is that your left hand can also grasp it when drawing and replacing the weapon. On the right side, you have to use one hand, which is also already holding the revolver, to try to open the cover and manage it. You can reach "left front" with both hands; "right rear," only with the right hand.

The revolver should never lie on its barrel in the holster, but always at the front, on the frame just before the cylinder. For this purpose, a thick piping must be sewn in, but this is important in any case, so that the barrel does not have to push apart the two leather halves when the weapon is inserted in the holster. This wears away only the browning and clamps the weapon uncontrollably tightly.

The belt loop should not be too narrow, but neither should it be too bulky, so that the holster is pulled tight to the belt and has little play. You have to make a compromise regarding the level of the belt loop on the holster: the higher the holster sits—and the lower the loop is sewn on—the more comfortably

It is best to draw the template on old hanging files; this is exactly the right material.

the holster sits, if the weapon is not given excess weight. The disadvantage, however, is that you then have to draw the weapon farther upward to get it free. The higher up the loop sits and the lower the holster hangs, the harder it is to wear. For this reason, you can get the weapon free with less arm movement and can thus draw faster. The low-sitting western holsters are inspired by the imagination of Hollywood scriptwriters and do not correspond to the historical models that developed in the daily work of cowboys or the cavalry.

The higher up the loop sits and the lower the holster hangs, the worse it is to wear.

MEASURING

When measuring, you should first work with coarse packing paper or a hanging file. Draw a line that corresponds to the visor line of the weapon and on which the leather is later placed. Then draw the outline of the weapon on the underside of the holster.

To be able to correctly mark the belt loop, hold the cutting pattern with the weapon right at the position on the belt where the holster is to sit later, and draw a line with a soft pencil along the top side of the belt, on the cutting pattern. You can use this to guide yourself later on. The loop goes downward, exactly there in the right angle. Where this will be later applied exactly is determined by the cutting pattern. The more at an angle the holster sits, the more difficult it becomes to find space for

Transfer the template to the leather.

Do not forget to draw on the centerline, where the leather will be folded later.

Trace the shape of the template and you can cut out the leather.

Cut out the piping and double it in the upper part.

the lower seam because the tip moves out of the perpendicular. If you are going to make the holster for a particular belt, then it is a good idea to adjust the belt loop to it exactly and to lay a leather sheath underneath to line it, so that the holster can move as little as possible. It is also sometimes helpful to design the holster on the lower side, where the barrel sticks in, to be wider than necessary and to thus gain a centimeter or so more space for the belt loop. You can conceal this with a double seam parallel to the seam at the edge of the leather.

The curvature of the revolver in the holster makes it difficult to calculate the allowance for the seam. Here, you should work more generously at first and opt to cut away a centimeter from the border of the holster, rather than be miserly and allow too little and have to discard the total cut piece because it came out too small. You can always cut off, but there is no way to "cut on." You can save a holster that is too small by using a thick piping, but only to a very small extent.

On the lower side of the holster, where the barrel mouth lies, you can sew in a drop-shaped piece of leather, but this already requires quite a bit of skill. For narrower barrels and a big-enough seam allowance, you can leave it with an intermediate layer in the seam—that should create enough space. On the back side, at the lowest end, punch in a hole so that water can drain off, or just don't sew the holster completely closed.

SEWING

When sewing the holster together, you should first work on the front side and make the groove for the seam. Then tack the holster together with nails and try out the fit. In this condition, you can still make changes to the underside, which you will not see later. When you have chamfered out the groove for the seam, it is too late. If it means you can see only a few nail holes on the back, you can still move the seam. Once everything fits and you are satisfied, pull out the nails again and make the groove for the seam, mark the hole intervals, craft the important edges, and sew on the belt loop. Depending on the cutting pattern, it may be that the button stud back is no longer accessible after sewing the holster together; then you have to mount it. Use a large drive punch to cut a round piece out of some soft, thin leather, and glue it over the stud, if this might come into contact with the revolver—this prevents scratching. The closer it sits to the seam, the more stable it is; if it is in the middle of the holster, it can become very unstable when the rigid leather cover is opened or buttoned closed.

Mark where the button stud hole is to go once, but do not punch a hole in the leather yet; this is done at the end, so the seam runs correctly.

Some contact adhesive can help you assemble the different parts; this is also recommended on large pieces. The important places are additionally held together with nails.

Now comes sewing the big seam. Here you should be economical with your last thread just when you are three stitches from the end. You should not use the last 4 inches (10 cm) of thread on the needle. On the one hand, the thread is very stressed and worn out there and is not well waxed, and on the other hand, you need a certain amount of thread to draw the knots and stitches tight. Here you should not save on a yard of thread.

If you want to set a rivet at the corner of the holster, which is not the worst idea, then end the seam appropriately sooner. In this case, however, you should use a sufficiently strong and wide intermediate layer so that there is also enough space for the rivet, and the rivet hole does not cut through the piping, and so that the rivet head doesn't extend over edge and, in the worst case, has to be sanded off. Thus there should always still be some leather on the edge from the rivet head outward. But the last stitch can disappear under the rivet head.

Once the seam has been completed, use the wheel to go over the stitches once again to press them downward and to level them. Use the cobbler's knife to cut off the remaining leather pieces smoothly. On such thick and long edges, a belt sander helps sand the leather layers flat. Use a fine belt to smooth the edges. Then chamfer the edge with an edge beveler and continue to work as described in detail elsewhere.

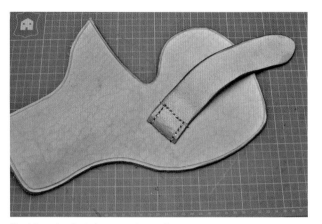

Fashion the belt loop and sew it on.

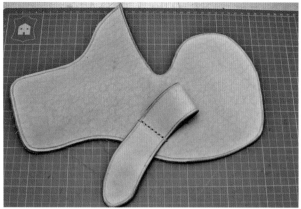

With the second seam, sew on the finished belt loop.

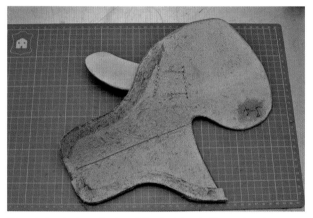

The piping is inserted and the holster is then glued together.

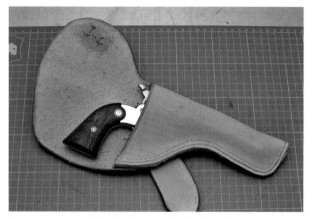

Now you can try the holster on for the first time; the seam is already prepared.

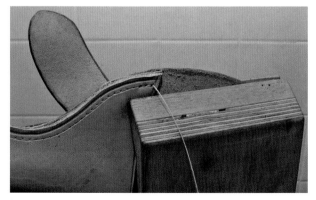

First sew back over the first three stitches, to make them hold better.

In some places, the holster is difficult to clamp in. In such places, you can hold a champagne cork against it.

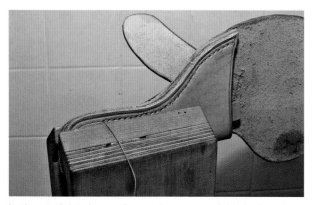

In the straight places, the sewing goes quickly by hand.

Mark the position of the fastener with an awl, but do not pierce through all the leather layers.

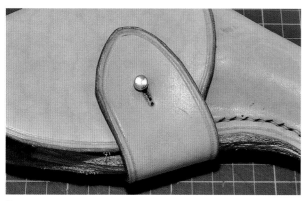

The button stud was inserted and the holster fits perfectly.

The edge is crafted to a finish.

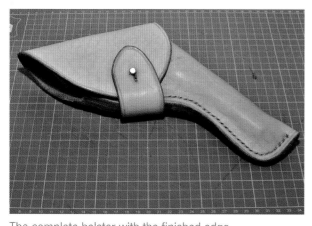

The complete holster with the finished edge.

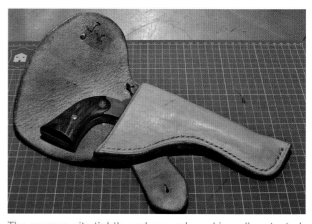

The weapon sits tightly and securely and is well protected.

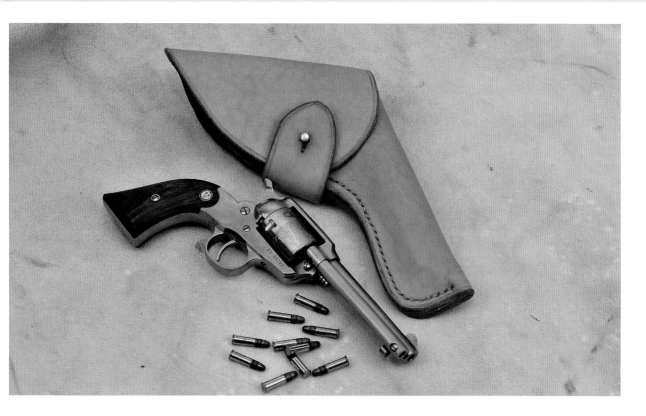

WET-FORMING

After it has been sewn, a holster is not optimally shaped to fit. For knives, which are rather flat, simply sewing the sheath together is usually sufficient, but this is not the case for revolvers. You need to soak the leather in water that is warm to the hand for a few seconds to make it soft and flexible. The water should penetrate only the outer layers and not soak through the leather completely. Then wrap the revolver in plastic wrap, to protect it from the aggressive tannic acid, and stick it in the holster. It usually slips a little deeper than you would like, and the button stud hole would no longer match. Press the leather on the revolver, especially under the cylinder, just where the weapon is to rest later on. The point here is just to press the leather somewhat against the weapon, but not to work the fluting of the cylinder into the grain side of the leather. This would be important to create a secure seat for a fast-draw holster, but here it is counterproductive. Leave the weapon in the holster and let it dry for one day. Check to make sure that the weapon, unwrapped from the plastic wrap, sits securely in the holster and does not wobble. Then check that the button stud hole will still sit in the right place, correct it if necessary, and punch out the big and small holes and connect them with a neat slit.

Recraft the edges and grease the holster lightly inside and out. Your first homemade holster is ready and will accompany you faithfully for many years.

For knives, which are rather flat, simply sewing the sheath together is usually sufficient, but this is not the case for revolvers.

Other Schiffer Books on Related Subjects

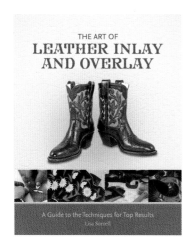

*THE ART OF LEATHER INLAY
AND OVERLAY:
A Guide to the Techniques for Top Results*
Lisa Sorrell
ISBN: 978-0-7643-5121-1

*TANNED LEATHER HAND-MADE BAGS:
Ultimate Techniques*
Yoko Ganaha and Piggy Tsujioka
ISBN: 978-0-7643-5612-4

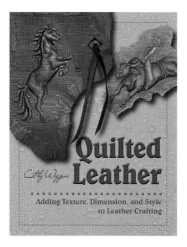

*QUILTED LEATHER:
Adding Texture, Dimension,
and Style to Leather Crafting*
Cathy Wiggins
ISBN: 978-0-7643-5500-4

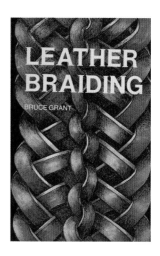

LEATHER BRAIDING
Bruce Grant
ISBN: 978-0-87033-039-1